PELICAN

SOVIET COMM
AGRARIAN RE

ROY D. LAIRD, who was av
University of Washington, is cu
Science at the University of K
staff of the Slavic and Soviet
Nebraska in 1925, he has com
ground with his interest in
reflected in his writing. He is
books and monographs and the
than fifty articles and book
Collective Farming in Russia, Th
as an Instrument of Soviet Rule, *Soviet Agricultural Affairs,*
and *Soviet Agriculture: The Permanent Crisis*. He has just
completed another book, *The Soviet Paradigm,* which will be
published in 1970. Professor Laird is the founder of the
Conference on Soviet Agriculture and Peasant Affairs. He
has won many awards including the Rockefeller Research
Fellowship, a National Science Foundation research grant
and an NDEA Fulbright-Hays research grant. He has
lectured on Soviet agriculture at many universities both in
the States and in Europe.

BETTY A. LAIRD, also from Nebraska and a graduate of
Hastings College there, has often assisted Professor Laird in
the past in editing his manuscripts. However, in the present
book she has taken an active part in writing it as well as
participating in the research in Mexico, Poland and Yugoslavia. She has taught English at the University of Kansas
for several years.

Professor and Mrs Laird have two sons and a daughter.

Soviet Communism and Agrarian Revolution

ROY D. AND BETTY A. LAIRD

PENGUIN BOOKS

Penguin Books Ltd, Harmondsworth, Middlesex, England
Penguin Books Inc., 7110 Ambassador Road, Baltimore, Maryland 21207, U.S.A.
Penguin Books Australia Ltd, Ringwood, Victoria, Australia

—

First published 1970

—

Copyright © Roy D. and Betty A. Laird, 1970

—

Made and printed in Great Britain by
C. Nicholls & Company Ltd
Set in Monotype Plantin

TO CLAUDE, DAVID AND HEATHER

Contents

CONTENTS

Part Three
INTERNATIONAL DIMENSIONS

Preface

THIS book was written out of concern over a mounting revolution sweeping that majority of mankind that lives in the rural areas of the developing nations.

The major problem threatening the future of mankind is two-headed. While on one side the population explosion is pushing mankind into ever more crowded areas, on the other the lagging growth in food production is leaving an ever widening gap between output and demand. Man will be confronted by a calamity of unprecedented proportions if birth rates do not decline and if food production is not increased at least to the point where not only the probability of mass starvation is removed, but present mass hunger and malnutrition are sharply reduced.

Specifically, this book concentrates upon the negative influences of communist doctrine and practice upon the crisis in food production, rooted as they are in false myths which have distorted or hidden an important part of the truth that must be faced if a calamity of world proportions is to be averted. Not only have the communist states failed to produce enough food, but if the accelerating world disaster in food production is to be halted, the communist example of creating huge collective and state farms must not be emulated by new Chinas and Cubas, developing nations opting for quick paths to economic success.

Unfortunately a strong link has formed between agricultural theory and practice in communist states and the agrarian revolution gathering force in other parts of the world. There are many reasons for this:

1. The majority of mankind lives in the developing nations of Asia, Africa and Latin America, where the economic pattern is predominantly rural. Most of their people are ill-housed, ill-clothed and (in spite of an agrarian life) ill-fed. Such mass misery has been the breeding ground of local communist leaders.

9

2. Whether communist or not, the leaders of the advancing tempo of revolutionary unrest, largely centred in these nations, see in the Soviet model great attractions.

3. Communist revolutions (to be contrasted with the takeover of the Eastern European states after the Second World War) have after all succeeded in predominantly agricultural societies.

4. Ironically, however, agriculture has been and remains the major domestic problem of communist states. Both the incumbent and the revolutionary political leadership, almost everywhere, is monopolized by urban leaders who have lost touch with, or never knew, the particular needs of rural peoples and the vital but special requirements of agricultural production. Urban-oriented communist leaders are particularly blind to the needs of agriculture.

In face of mankind's dire need for more food, too many communist policies have been disastrously counterproductive, because they have been rooted in misconceptions of the needs of agriculture, which in turn are derived from what Professor Robert MacIver would call 'false myths'. As he stresses in his modern classic, *The Web of Government*, myths can be true or false, scientifically verifiable or based upon pure superstition. Nevertheless, however derived, in sum they comprise 'the value-impregnated beliefs and notions that men hold, that they live by or live for'. As he further notes, 'all social relations, the very texture of human society, are myth born and myth sustained'.[1]* Here, we are concerned with doctrines that have guided communist societies in making agricultural policy, false myths that go counter to scientific discovery yet have become so deeply ingrained in men's minds that even after new evidence has pointed in a different direction, old habits and views persist. Such are the sources of much that demands change in communist agricultural systems. Such are the sources of policies and practices that must not be copied by the developing nations, if they are to carry out their much needed agrarian revolutions in ways that will assure increased food production in an ill-fed world.

Any work that attempts a high level of scholarly accuracy owes a great debt to the writings of many colleagues. Specifically,

* References are listed on pp. 130–36.

we wish to thank Professor Anna M. Cienciala of the University of Kansas and Professor Joel M. Halpern of the University of Massachusetts for many helpful suggestions arising out of their reading an early draft of the work. A complete list of those whose work has helped us would include scores of scholars, but at the least we must note Drs Naum Jasny and Lazar Volin, great pioneers in the field of Soviet agricultural studies whose work is now done, but never to be forgotten. Much of the material presented here is a result of decades of research, for which the generous support of the University of Kansas deserves much credit. From 1966 to 1968, however, National Science Foundation and NDEA Fulbright research grants made the Mexican and Eastern European comparative study possible. Finally I would like to thank Betty Laird, on many earlier occasions editorial assistant, for her help in field research and her active participation as co-author.

Lawrence, Kansas, 1969   ROY D. LAIRD

CHAPTER I

Foreword

THE twentieth century is the century of rural revolution. If United Nations survey figures are correct in implying that over fifty per cent of the world's population still remains rural,[1] this world-wide agrarian revolution may have a greater impact on mankind than did the urban-centred industrial revolution of the nineteenth century. Ironically, most political leaders and intellectuals in the developed nations are ignorant of agriculture's particular needs and problems. In the United States and the USSR, in particular, most of the wealth and most of the key positions of political power are now held by urban-reared and industrially oriented leaders who view the rural scene through lenses clouded by industrial smog, and the false and misleading myths about agriculture and rural life that they perpetrate must be recognized as a major source of the world's agricultural problems.

PEASANT!

One common false myth is that peasants tend to be stupid, impassive clods, frequently drunk, and that they are neither intelligent enough nor ambitious enough to do anything but till the soil. Impassive and stubborn they may be – an old Russian proverb quoted in Ivan Turgenev's *Fathers and Sons* is probably applicable to farmers the world over: 'A Russian peasant will get the better of God himself.' But these characteristics, however typical, are born of a need to cope with great adversity and should never be mistaken for either a lack of intelligence or a satisfaction with rural slums and ghettoes. Some peasants undoubtedly drink too much, but is it any wonder? Drunkenness is often a symptom of deep dissatisfaction with one's lot, implying a seething torment that can be dissolved only in several ounces of vodka or home brew. Finally, there is the implication that managing a farm requires no intelligence, that therefore normal people have no desire to farm. Although the idyllic life has long been a favourite subject for painters and poets, who have praised the colours of nature, the warmth of animals, the sounds and smells of creation and growth, the satisfaction of being able to hold and measure the produce of one's physical and mental efforts, it is not often realized that a substantial portion of that produce is the direct result of intelligent planning and timely altering of plans for changing circumstances, as well as of backbreaking labour. Unfortunately, peasants do receive less formal education than most city people, but their seeming lack of sophistication should not be mistaken for general stupidity or ignorance. Indeed, if they were to change places, the peasant would probably fare better in a city environment than would his city-bred cousin on the farm.

'INDUSTRIAL FUNDAMENTALISM'

Perhaps the most encompassing of the false myths about agriculture is the gross misconception about the impact of the industrial revolution on rural activity. Professor T. W. Schultz, in his book *Transforming Traditional Agriculture*, describes this distorted faith in technological advance as 'industrial fundamentalism'.[2]

Industry has had an enormous impact on modern farming in the developed nations, but this cannot be equated with the impact of the industrial revolution on urban production. The early artisan of the cities employed few, relatively simple, hand-powered tools. Most importantly, the finished product was primarily the work of the individual craftsman. The cabinet maker, for example, though helped by apprentices, usually made a piece of furniture by himself from start to finish. In contrast, modern industry produces countless objects for the consumer with no stamp of individual workmanship. With the advance of automation, more and more items reach the market without ever having been touched by human hands or even seen by human eyes.

Of course, a farmer with modern machines will touch few of his individual plants. Yet his role in the production process has not changed essentially. As two leading students of American agriculture, John M. Brewster and Gene Wunderlich, have emphasized, there has been no agricultural industrial revolution. 'With minor exceptions of certain specialized poultry and livestock operations, a shift to machine farming leaves relatively undisturbed the sequential pattern of operations that has prevailed in farming since the domestication of plants and animals.... Thus, in farming the "Industrial Revolution" is merely a spectacular change in the gadgets with which operations are performed, whereas in industry it is a fundamental revolution in the sequence of productive operations.'[3] A number of urban misconceptions about agriculture can be traced directly to a failure to recognize this.

First of all, there is a widespread failure to see the great discrepancy between industrial and agricultural growth rates. Prior to the industrial revolution this discrepancy must have been very small. Today, however, the world rate of industrial growth is more than two and a half times that of agricultural growth, and, moreover, this difference seems to be affected very little (if at all) by the level of a nation's industrial development. These observations are confirmed by world-wide data,* as illustrated in Table 1 below, reflecting agricultural v. industrial growth for both the developing and developed nations.

* These calculations are based upon the United Nations 'Index Numbers of Gross Domestic Product by Industrial Origin, World Excluding USSR and Eastern Europe'. The developed countries include 'North America, Europe, Oceania, together with Japan and South Africa'. The developing countries include 'Latin America, Asia and the Far East (except Japan), and the Middle East and Africa (except South Africa)'.[4]

Table 1

RELATIVE RATES OF GROWTH:
AGRICULTURE *v.* INDUSTRY 1958–63
(1958 = 100)

Adapted from *Statistical Yearbook, 1965*,
United Nations, New York, 1966, p. 27.

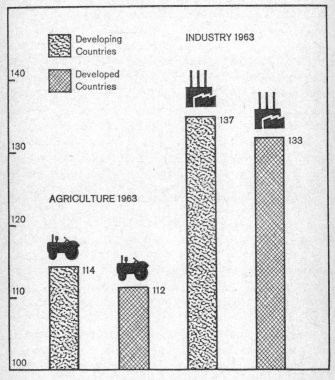

Another important misconception is that chemical fertilizers and modern machines for applying them inevitably produce the maximum yield per acre. In fact, although they almost always result in significant labour savings, and do greatly increase yields, they do not always produce the best yield possible. In many instances chemical fertilizer, for example, is not as effective as natural fertilizer, or a combination of the two. Mechanization often leads to farm specialization, which means many modern farms keep no livestock and save on labour, but much of the land is left without any natural fertilizer.

It is also assumed that machine cultivation and harvesting of crops increase yields because they reduce weeds more rapidly and speed up the harvest. However, given ample and eager labour, human hands will pull weeds next to a plant that machines could not touch, and in hungry nations gleaners still stoop to pick up the fallen grain that machines would miss. Similarly, Asian farmers often reseed small gaps in their fields, which a machine could not detect, in order to squeeze out of the precious earth every possible gram of produce.

Centralized industrial management practice is said to have greatly enhanced farm production, particularly in the United States. Yet, with the major exception of the broiler industry, where chicken raising has been satisfactorily organized along industrial lines, this is not so. Students of contemporary American farming do stress that success or failure has become more and more dependent upon the farmer's business sense, but there is another difference: on the farm, management is directly involved in production and is not in some remote centralized office. Markets must be followed carefully, but success is a matter of responding to new economic opportunities by fitting them to the farm's particular potential, which depends in turn upon an intimate knowledge of the constantly changing physical environment on each acre of the land. Misunderstandings concerning modern American farm management (particularly in Soviet minds set upon huge industrially organized farms) lead to the belief that industrial farms are taking over in America. True, the average farm has more than doubled in size in recent decades, but crucial evidence (see Chapter 6 below) indicates that there are important limits on size, varying with the type of farm, if peak efficiency in management and production is to be maintained. This may well be why the huge corporate farms that do exist have actually declined in recent years and their share of the total output has diminished. The old family farm is believed to be rapidly disappearing from the American scene. Yet what might be described as the new family farm, but is probably more aptly characterized as the 'manager-operated farm', is in the ascendancy, and these new farms are not corporate industrial activities. On average they are much larger than before. Furthermore, much of the land is rented or farmed on shares with the owner rather than being owned by the manager-operator. However, the essence of the arrangement is that the person who makes key production and business decisions also is the key farm worker. The most important source of additional labour is other members of the family.

Most urban dwellers assume that modern equipment allows a farmer to impose industrial production controls over his production. True, chemical insecticides and herbicides do allow him more control over the farm environment than he enjoyed a few decades ago, yet the factory of farming is still the entire outdoors. Numerous natural changes which can profoundly affect output remain beyond the farmer's control. It is most unlikely that the rigidly controlled production environment that is essential for industrial success can ever be imposed on the roofless production plant of the farmer.

The American farmer is believed to produce more food than any other farmer in the world. When measured in terms of the number of mouths he feeds, which is nearly forty,[5] he is unequalled. However, American agriculture is a highly extensive system that evolved from a land-rich, labour-poor environment. When success is measured in output per acre of land, a crucial yardstick in most nations, American agriculture proves rather poor. Much of the world, especially Western Europe and

Japan, produces sometimes as much as three times more food per acre. Some of the differences in yields can be explained by soil and climate conditions, but much more important to the high production rate of Western European agriculture is their intensive system of cultivation. Farm labour is less expensive and in many cases, if given time, can do a job more thoroughly than can a complex machine. Crops are carefully rotated, natural fertilizer, composts of manure and vegetable matter, is applied to the maximum, and as a result yields are high.

There has certainly been a revolution in American agriculture in recent decades, but the misconceptions about its nature must be challenged. Well-meaning Soviet politicians looking for ways to improve food output, and goodwill emissaries to the USSR (for example, the Iowa farmer, Roswell Garst) and to other agriculturally backward nations have been too successful in convincing others that American technology can increase output in the food-short world. Of course American-developed fertilizers and hybrid seeds can have enormous value. However, Khrushchev understood the American example so poorly that he championed growing corn* over much of the USSR when, actually, relatively little of Russia's land has a climate suitable for this crop. Similarly, Western tractors may be of great value to India in making deep ploughing possible, but tractors produce only exhaust fumes, not manure, and if they are used valuable fertilizer will be lost.

American technology may be of use to other agricultural systems if it is applied with caution and with full understanding of the true agricultural revolution in the US. Let us examine that revolution by focussing on a specific area, that which the authors know best, as an example of the change wrought across the vast plains area of the United States since the 1930s.

* i.e. maize.

THE AMERICAN REVOLUTION:
THE NEBRASKA EXAMPLE

'There is no place like Nebraska . . .' is the first line of the Nebraska state song, but although the state is unique in many ways, the agrarian revolution that has occurred in Nebraska has been repeated (if in different form) in Texas, Idaho, Kentucky and most of the major agricultural regions of North America.

Nebraska was settled by peasant immigrants from Eastern and Northern Europe. As described by Willa Cather in what this plainsman regards as the greatest American novel, *My Antonia*, many hamlets were colonies of transplanted Czechs, Poles, Swedes, Danes or Germans, and all was not milk and honey. Roy Laird's mother and her brothers were born in a dugout in the hills of northwestern Nebraska under conditions that seemed desperate even for peasants who had emigrated from the poverty of Czechoslovakia. Sturdy sod houses were palaces in comparison to some of the Nebraska settlers' first homes. Although born in America, the brothers could not speak English when they started school. Even among adults who were knowledgeable in their native literature, few could read English well, and almost all spoke the new language with a heavy accent. Certainly few Nebraska farmers of the early 1900s had the knowledge or ability to communicate with the political and financial leadership in their new country. In many ways they were worse off than they had been at home, since they were now not only unschooled peasants, but peasants in a strange environment.

The Czech grandfather was a courageous, enormously hard-working man, but he had no money to buy good land (cheap as it was) and did not know how to find out how best to farm the steep and arid clay hills which became his farm. Very little if any of his land should have been broken to a plough, yet he attempted to grow corn on hillsides that washed away in the infrequent but heavy cloudbursts. Happily, what was his farm has now been returned to natural grasses and cattle grazing, the purpose for which it was always best suited. Perhaps, if he could have read more widely in English, he might have turned to managing profitably a small herd of cattle on his and his son's adjoining land, but he had only his Eastern European experience and tradition to go on, and this dictated the cultivation of grains.

The combined drought and depression of the 1930s hit Nebraska, which had little by way of natural resources other than agriculture, as hard as any state in the Union. The effects of the man-made depression, its devastation greatly increased by a drought that was natural, were considerably worsened by human ignorance and error. As on the grandfather's farm, hundreds of thousands of acres in the high plains states were cultivated that should never have been put to the plough, or if seeded should have been cultivated differently, by terracing hillside fields and contour ploughing, which then were virtually unheard of. When the dry southern winds came in the late summer sometimes the air was choked with a red dust, and we knew our lungs were filling with land loosened by Oklahoma ploughs. Other days the sky would be yellow with Texas soils. The more common black and grey drifts of dust that piled high behind buildings and snow fences was native Nebraska earth. The dryness provided ideal breeding conditions for jack-rabbits and especially grasshoppers. What plants survived the searing heat, when for weeks the temperature stayed over the 100s even at night, could be destroyed in a day's feasting by predatory insects and animals.

In the years when the sparse rains did come at fortuitous times, the prices paid for the crop hardly seemed worth the effort. Corn, which sold for some $1.12 a bushel in 1967, still too low a price, went as low as 15c a bushel. Matches, kerosene for the lamps, and the few other town supplies that could be afforded, were had by the exchange of pitiful handfuls of eggs and other produce bartered at the village store. The country doctor was paid in chickens and milk, if he was paid at all, and services that could not be paid for in produce were usually done without.

Many farmers, including some Scottish relatives, went West. The Czech grandfather lost his farm, and his oldest son, who was to have inherited the land, never shook off the despair that settled over him during the years when the sky was darkened by clouds of locusts and dust more often than it was with rain. Angry farmers increasingly expressed their wrath, communist organizers received a sympathetic hearing in the railway towns along the Union Pacific Railroad, veterans marched on Washington, soup kitchens were established in rural Nebraska, destitute farmers who were losing their land were nearing the point of joining forces with the urban poor, and America came as close as any industrial nation has to a red revolution.

Franklin Delano Roosevelt was first elected president in 1932, and although a conservative Supreme Court declared his National Recovery Act unconstitutional, he found increasing political support for his urban and agrarian reform programmes. Roosevelt was overwhelmingly returned in 1936, conservative agrarian Nebraska went Democratic (and not again until it rejected Goldwater in 1964), and agrarian Kansas unprecedentedly re-elected its New Deal Democratic Senator, George McGill. Nebraska's own George Norris had been a Republican, but he was independent, and the Norris Dam in the Tennessee Valley is fitting monument to his fight for rural conservation and reconstruction. Roosevelt was not all that liberal when he started his tenure as the nation's leader, but he rapidly learned that his own political survival and the survival of American democracy depended upon the creation of economic, and especially agricultural, policies that would serve to right the human errors that had been responsible for America's disastrous decline.

In spite of the totalitarian tendencies in Marx's doctrines, lessons borrowed from him and other European radicals combined with American pragmatism to produce an American socialism. The evolution of the more semantically palatable 'welfare state' in the United States, and Western Europe's evolution of socialist labour parties, that combined state action with the free ballot and the free press, must be regarded as one of the greatest successes of the democratic tradition. Calling a spade a spade, we should recognize Franklin Roosevelt's 'New Deal' as the beginning of American socialism, but socialism which carried with it an insistence upon retaining democratic rule. The key to rural recovery lay in policies that could be coordinated only by a strong federal government. At the same time that Stalin was forcing Russia's peasants into collective and state farms in what he admitted was a 'revolution from above', Nebraska (and most of rural America) inaugurated its own agrarian revolution. The leadership and coordinating effort came primarily from Washington, D.C., but persuasion, economic assistance and the ballot, rather than force, were the techniques used.

The pragmatic American socialism called the 'New Deal' was a revolution led from above that succeeded because it prompted eager cooperation from those below. Price support programmes, although still set too low, promised that grain prices would never again fall to depression levels. Enormous federal (and sometimes state) investments built numerous huge reservoirs for combined flood control, irrigation and recreation along Nebraska's Platte and Republican rivers. Mile upon mile of windbreaking shelter belts were planted, and loose and hilly soils were replanted to native grasses. The complex of ditch irrigation systems begun then is still being expanded, and where the land is too rolling to be levelled with huge land levelling machines, hundreds of thousands of deep-well irrigation systems combined with sprinkler pipes bring water to the fields. On today's farm seeds are hybrid, soils have been tested, and investment in machinery and buildings can easily run beyond $100,000. Land that sold in 1934 for twenty dollars an acre may now be worth nearly a thousand dollars.

Enormous road building and improvement programmes put the unemployed to work and transformed the countryside, so that most Nebraska farmers now have access to town markets in only a few minutes on all-weather roads. In communist countries not one of these major rural development programmes could avoid being acclaimed as a great contribution of authoritarian socialism. Yet one would have to look hard to find a Nebraska farmer who would not bridle if told that he has benefited tremendously from the fruits of democratic socialism. Asked to characterize the many federal programmes he now takes for granted he would stoutly assert that they are justly paid for by his taxes. Thanks largely to the federal Rural Electrification Association, some 98 per cent of today's Nebraska farmers have electricity, but such programmes are not seen as socialistic, just as good sense.[6]

Most important of all the new government programmes, however, have been those that transformed the farmer himself. Fortunately many, perhaps most, of the illiterate immigrants tended to view education as the most precious of all gifts they could give their children. A diploma from a tax-supported high school came to be viewed as a birthright. Moreover, today most of the grandchildren of the original immigrants have attended one of the state's colleges and universities, of which there are more than a score. Their fees are much lower than the actual cost of their education, and most students receive one form or another of tax-supported (but non-'socialistic') assistance as well. Like the rest of the nation, Nebraska is rapidly coming to regard a college degree also as a birthright for those who want and can benefit from the experience.

The GI Bills passed after the Second World War, that paid for a veteran's higher education, have meant that among the Nebraska farmers under fifty the average probably has some two years of college training, and many are graduates of the

University of Nebraska's College of Agriculture, created by a federal land grant. Certainly, the great majority of them have the high level of technical and business knowledge that is essential to farm successfully. When a farmer puts on his suit – and he does today – no one can pick him out of a city crowd and point to him as a man of the soil. These alterations in the farmer himself, much more than the changes in his land and equipment, make him seem much more than just two generations removed from his European peasant grandfathers who were losing the struggle with the soil some three decades ago.

The county agent (paid by federal funds), formerly regarded with suspicion, serves as liaison between the farmer and the government, explaining policies and providing valuable information and suggestions to those who ask for them. There are available thousands of government pamphlets containing the latest information on hybrid seeds, soil quality, weed control, cattle breeding, and almost every phase of farming. Associations such as the Grange, the Future Farmers of America and the 4H have become important social, educational and political institutions in the life of the farmer.

There is much more to the American agricultural revolution. All areas have not been as fortunate as Nebraska. Many farmers, such as the Czech grandfather, were unable to hang on to their land. Nevertheless, no war against America's peasants was fought, and most of them have profited enormously. Socialism is a tainted word in Nebraska, but ask a Nebraska farmer over fifty to describe the changes in his lifetime and along with his conservative-sounding doctrines he may well point to the nearest shelterbelt and refer to it as a monument to FDR.

When the USSR and other rurally underdeveloped nations send delegations to the United States to learn the secrets of its agricultural success and these delegations see only the new machines, the hybrid seeds and the chemicals, unaware of the context in which they see them, the impressions they return home with are highly distorted. As vital as these new gadgets may seem, since the production process remains essentially unchanged, gaining full benefits from new technology primarily depends upon the farmer and the assistance he receives from outside, especially governmental agencies. A failure to see the changes in the farmer, along with the changes in society, and changes in the relationship of the farmer to government so that a new partnership in production has been created, is to miss the essence of the American agrarian revolution.

That the newly evolved government–farmer partnership is vital can be documented again and again. For example, the classification of soils and creation of watersheds are primary government contributions to the partnership. The key role of the county agent has already been described. Many dairy farmers depend on federally supplied power for their milking machines and silage cutters. Much of the irrigated corn would be ruined by a few days of searing July heat if the electrically driven well pumps were to fail. Some of the most dedicated of government employees in a state like Nebraska are Rural Electrification Association linemen who turn out all hours of the day and night in every kind of weather to repair storm-damaged power lines and maintain the supply to the farmer.

Although the United States can hardly take credit or blame for the original decision of the Soviet Union to adopt an extensive collectivized system, communist (and Western) misreadings of the nature of American agricultural successes have contributed to Soviet insistence on pursuing agricultural practices that are economically disastrous. Most certainly, evidence from Soviet and especially Polish practice indicates that the price of collectivization is not only dissatisfaction among farmers but also an enormous waste of labour and a loss in food output that may be more than fifteen per cent of the possible maximum. Causes for this waste are not economic, but stem from distorted beliefs that ignore problems of farm organization and management as related to size, and from central interference in farm decision-making.

Ironically, agricultural delegations from communist and some underdeveloped nations seem to be blind to the human rural revolution which they so badly need, and they try to copy the American labour-saving technology which they may not need at all if they are land-short and labour-rich. The price American farmers pay in lost yields for their extensive cultivation makes complete economic sense as long as food surpluses remain a major problem. American farm specialization is enormously efficient for her needs, but for most developing nations that need to make the most of limited soil resources, less specialized farms, more careful rotation, and balancing crops and livestock may be more efficient ways of gaining the maximum production of food from the land.

Unfortunately, although the post-Khrushchev leadership in the USSR correctly concluded that greater yields per hectare must be realized on established Soviet farm lands, the new leadership will probably be disappointed in the results of its new 'intensification' programme. Great increases in mineral fertilizer production and expansion of the area of irrigated land will no doubt bring important benefits, but every indication is that the new policies still incorporate a vision of huge, essentially extensive farms that, however different in organization from United States farms, are still closer to the American system than to the high-yielding Western European or Japanese intensive cultivation.

The nature of modern industrial production is such that whole factories can be successfully transported over thousands of miles by boat and rail. Such imports can revolutionize urban production. Tractors and chemical fertilizers also are easily transported, but they are not the essence of successful agrarian revolutions, which must institute social and political changes in the farmers themselves.

Part One

POLITICS AND MYTH

CHAPTER 2

The Politics of Stalin's 'Revolution from Above'

JUST as 'there is no place like Nebraska', so there is no place quite like the rural USSR with its huge collective and state farms. The reformation that has divided the communist world into increasingly independent nationalist-communist states is very real, yet there are enough similarities in the agricultural policies and problems of most communist nations for an appraisal of agriculture in the USSR to carry wide implications. True, in 'the great leap forward' of 1959, the Chinese attempted and miserably failed to go beyond the Soviet Union and directly into agricultural communes, with total communal living and without the private home and plots that are so important to the Eastern European and Soviet peasant. As important exceptions, Poland and Yugoslavia refused to slavishly adopt the forced, fully collectivized Soviet model, and only some fifteen per cent of their agriculture is collectivized, made up of state and collective farms mostly created from huge estates taken over from former landlords. Elsewhere the agrarian revolution imposed by Stalin on the Soviet peasant in the early 1930s has been copied by other communist states.

From both humanitarian and practical standpoints the pre-revolutionary agrarian systems, emphatically in Tsarist Russia, were highly unsatisfactory. The few plots that the landlords left to the peasants for them to eke out a living were too fragmented for efficient cultivation. Many, if not most, of the landowners did not maximize the output from their holdings. In theory the Russian peasants had been politically emancipated from serfdom in 1861, but because of the unjust distribution of the land, the great bulk of the peasantry, who comprised the vast majority of the population, remained virtual slaves of the local lords. Tsarist agrarian policies forced the peasant revolution that came on the heels of the losses to Germany in the First World War. Surely, given the hardships and special problems of the early years, for most of its agrarian policies between the revolution and the end of the 1920s the Bolshevik leadership cannot be seriously faulted. After Stalin's closing of the NEP (New Economic Policy) in 1928, however, Western observers can and do raise serious questions about the course of subsequent policies, which were largely Stalinist.

In 1913 more than 80 per cent of the Russian population was rural. By 1966, since more peasants than could be accounted for by the growth of the rural population had gone to the cities, only 46 per cent of the population (107 out of a total of 232 million) remained classified as rural.* There has been a comparable shift in output. Since the Second World War the USSR has gained a place as the world's second greatest industrial power, but only at the cost of creating a complex problem in agriculture, the magnitude of which was dramatized by the drought of 1963. Whereas Tsarist Russia had been a major exporter of grain, 1963 was but the first year of many that the Soviet Union imported large quantities of grain. Indeed, a projection of future needs (summarized in Chapter 5 below) implies that the USSR can be expected to remain a net importer of foodstuffs for the forseeable future.[3]

Agriculture remains the most important Soviet domestic economic problem. Although causes for this state of affairs rest in history, economics and geography, probably political demands on the rural USSR, more than any other factor, may

* Interestingly, the absolute reduction of the Soviet rural population has been relatively small, from 130·7 million in 1913 to 107·1 million in 1966. (This in fact is a slight increase on the 1897 figure of 106·2 million.[1]) Indeed, there is an important contrast between the USSR and other highly industrialized societies, where the proportion of rural population to urban tends to be much smaller.[2]

be credited with the disappointing advances in food production. Politics, in this context, encompasses the particular demands of institutions of rule, and the beliefs that may guide governmental decision-makers, that can influence the actions of a First Secretary of the CPSU or a chairman of a collective farm, and which go beyond the mere exercise (or threat) of force that is implied in many definitions of politics. Unlike the urban setting, where most workers live in two quite separate environments during their work and their off-duty hours, agriculture tends to be a comprehensive way of life. Under any economic system, most farms are not only basic production units, but primary social units at the same time. However, where collectivization has been established, the farm unit of a Soviet *kolkhoz*, an Israeli *kibbutz* or a Mexican collective *ejido* encompasses the primary unit of local government as well.

LENIN AND THE THIRD REVOLUTION

Most existing descriptions of the events of 1917 tend to concentrate on only one, or at most two, of the three revolutions that occurred in 1917, that is, on the downfall of Tsardom in the spring and the successful seizure of the central reins of power by the Bolsheviks in the fall. Far too little attention is given to the third revolution of that year, without which the other two could not have been possible. Surely, Tsardom would not have fallen when it did if the predominantly peasant army had not decided that it no longer could support the old regime. Surely, Bolshevism would never have come to power had not a peasant (largely spontaneous) revolution occurred throughout the countryside. Starting early in the year, in region after region the peasants arose, cast out the landlords, burned many of the manorhouses and seized the land. True, the end of centuries of Tsarist rule and the beginning of the Soviet experiment in communist rule were momentous happenings. Moreover, the Bolsheviks' genius for organization and the

33

Russian defeats at the hands of the Germans during the First World War were also decisive. But the events of 1917 were surely determined by the inadequacies of the 1861 emancipation; certainly the course became unchangeable when the 'Stolypins',* or agrarian reforms, of 1906–11 proved to be too little and far too late. The peasant seizure of the countryside was the major revolution, whereas the Bolshevik takeover marked only the beginning of a highly tenuous, largely urban adventure. Even in the cities the Bolsheviks were not assured of control until after three years of civil war, and the rural areas remained more or less dominated by the peasants until the early 1930s and Stalin's successful 'revolution from above' – his own description of forced collectivization.

After the brief 1918 'honeymoon' from fighting, 'War Communism' broke into the open, and again peasant attitudes were the key to the outcome. Of course, peasant allegiances were divided between the Reds and the Whites, and many undoubtedly wished a plague on both the warring houses. Nevertheless, the Bolsheviks could hardly have triumphed had they not succeeded in identifying the Red cause in many peasant minds with the seizure of the land from the landlords. Bolshevik slogans and early Soviet legislation supported the peasants' actions. In contrast many peasants, often rightly, identified White forces with those elements that would reinstate the landlords.†

* Stolypin was the Tsarist Prime Minister from 1906 until his assassination in 1911.

† Twentieth-century communists are much more than just agrarian reformers. Indeed, once power is seized, industrialization at the highest possible speed tends to become the primary objective. Nevertheless, the basic pattern established in 1917 has been repeated in subsequent revolutionary takeovers. China, Yugoslavia, Vietnam and Cuba were all predominantly peasant societies that have followed revolutionary paths similar to that of Russia in 1917.

THE 'PEASANT BREST-LITOVSK'[4]

Although the limited peasant cooperation with the Reds had been key to the defeat of the Whites and the interventionists, some of the new leaders wanted to carry the revolution to the countryside in 1921. However, as early as March 1919, Lenin found it necessary to admonish some of the more zealous comrades for attempting to force collectivization upon the peasants when he believed different tactics were needed.

The Bolsheviks had captured the key cities in 1917, and by 1921 they had won the civil war. Now, however, there appeared grave signs that the convenient alliance of the peasant and communist revolutions was about to come apart, and in a way that could destroy the new political system. Peasant uprisings were increasing alarmingly. These were climaxed by a revolt of the sailors in the former Tsarist garrison at Kronstadt (who had given important support to the Bolsheviks in 1917) against the communist rule. More than this, much of the food needed by the cities was not forthcoming from the countryside. The mounting catastrophe resulted in Lenin's call, in effect, to go in the opposite direction from collectivization by adopting his NEP (New Economic Policy) in 1921, as the solution to both the serious political threat from the peasants and the growing economic problem rooted in agriculture.[5]

The increasing possibility that an aroused peasantry could provide the base for a counter-revolutionary force was undoubtedly the primary consideration behind Lenin's decision to free the rural economy, by such measures as substituting a tax in kind for forced requisitions and freeing the trade in foodstuffs from earlier restrictions, measures that promoted peasant independence. Nevertheless, beyond the political threat of the new regime, Lenin's taking of 'one step backward [from communism] for two [later] steps forward' also served to alleviate an increasingly serious economic problem, one that Trotsky aptly described in 1922 as resulting in a 'scissors crisis'. 1922 provided a good harvest, which might have contributed to the alleviation of the urban food problem. However, by the time of the 1923 harvest the 'terms of trade' between the town and the countryside had become so bad from the peasants' point of view that the inflated roubles they were paid for their grain bought precious little of the ever more scarce goods of industry. Indeed, when food prices were compared with industrial prices, prices had changed places from the relative position they had held earlier. Thus, looking at a chart reflecting this cross-over, Trotsky described the ever-widening gap between prices paid for the peasants' produce and the cost of urban goods as similar to the opening blades of a pair of scissors. Not only had the peasants shown an alarming increase in counter-revolutionary attitudes, but their response to the mounting economic problem was to eat more of their food while growing less for the cities. Fortunately for the survival of the new experiment, the NEP not only calmed the peasants politically, but in a few years the 'one step backwards' had stimulated a significant recovery in food production.

Lenin's NEP was, however, only a temporary measure, and he never gave up his conviction that the eventual success of the communist experiment demanded bringing communism to the countryside as well as to the cities. In his famous assertion, 'Communism is the Soviet power plus the electrification of the whole country', he expressed his belief that electrification would provide 'a large-scale industrial basis' in agriculture, whereby machine production means and industrial management methods would enable the construction of rural communism.[6] Collectivization was Lenin's ultimate goal, but one that he believed could be achieved only voluntarily. Unlike many other communists, Lenin saw that unless the peasants recognized the (asserted) superiority of industrial farming, the willingness needed to operate the farms successfully would be lacking. Lenin repeated the importance of collectivization being voluntary time and again.[7]* What might have been the course of agricultural policy had he not died in 1924 can never be known. Yet the Leninist NEP that prevailed from 1921 to 1928 prescribed two Russias. The urban industrial centres were nationalized, socialized, and brought under close political control, while, in contrast, the countryside was adjusting to a landlordless system in a relatively anarchical political setting, during a period which some of the peasantry were later to describe as the 'golden era of Soviet rule'.[8]

FORCED COLLECTIVIZATION

By 1928 the first major crisis in agricultural production was past. Industrial output had also forged ahead. The time was ripe for a major policy change. Stalin, intent upon pushing up the industrial growth rate as rapidly as possible, now acted on his conviction that collective farms would extract the maximum investment capital from the countryside, and decided to create them by force. His motives seem to have been primarily economic, but powerful political and ideological considerations must also have been involved. More than a decade had passed since the revolution in the name of communism, yet agriculture remained outside the 'socialist' sphere. Since political theory is so important for communists, Stalin could hardly have launched his drive to build 'socialism in one state' while allowing the great bulk of the citizenry to remain in a 'capitalist' rural setting. Nor could he afford politically to disregard their enormous potential as a source of opposition without devising some means of control. If, however, Bolshevism could design and manage the institutions of rural organization,

* For this reason alone, Yugoslavia and Poland's decision to retain predominantly private agricultural systems can be described as much more correctly Leninist than the path of forced collectivization followed by the USSR and most other communist states.

perhaps the danger of trouble in the future could be eliminated.

Forced collectivization involved great hazards. As was implied in Stalin's famed 'Dizzy with Success' speech in 1930,[9] the drive could have boomeranged and encouraged organized opposition from the peasantry. Initially it depended upon harnessing the discontented and desperate peasants to the cause, through such acts as reviving the hard to control 'committees of the poor',* but it did not finally succeed until the Machine-Tractor Stations had been set up as the key to maintaining control over the *kolkhozy*.[10]

Lenin originated the 'committees of the poor' during War Communism, for this struggle would have been lost to the Whites if the grain necessary to feed the Red Army had not been successfully requisitioned from the peasantry. Lenin ingeniously devised the committees as the prime collection agent for this task. Who better than the hungry and jealous neighbours of a more fortunate peasant could know the location of his hidden grain? In a desperate final attempt to salvage Tsardom, Prime Minister Stolypin had wagered, and lost, on a policy of promoting the 'sturdy and the strong' element of the peasantry as a base of support for the government. Lenin, in turn, saved Bolshevism by sending a relatively small handful of disciplined comrades into the countryside to harness the forces of the needy (and the drunken). During forced collectivization, Stalin employed the same divide-and-conquer means for bringing the peasants into the *kolkhozy*. More than a decade of persuasion had failed to advance socialized agriculture voluntarily. Surely, no army could have been found to herd the peasants on to the state farms. However, peasant 'committees of the poor' who were told to set upon the *kulaks* (literally 'hard fist', that is, the rich peasants) turned the trick. Some of the victims of the drive had been relatively rich peasants who had exploited the labour of poorer farmers, but many of the peasants branded as *kulaks* were little or no better

* See also Chapter 7 below.

off than the rest. Some peasants undoubtedly were dispossessed as a result of a neighbour's wish to settle an old grudge.

The immediate price of Stalin's policy of compulsory collectivization was man-made famine. Millions lost their lives. So many of the peasants destroyed their animals rather than take them into the hated collectives that the cattle herds did not reach the 1928 level again until well into the 1950s. Field work was almost universally disrupted. Nevertheless, by the early 1930s most of the peasants were in collectives. Though there were continuing production losses due to the inefficiencies of the huge collective and state farms, the tactic was enormously successful in fulfilling Stalin's major purposes of the time. 'Committees of the poor', however, like most instruments of revolution, were only temporary tools unsuited for continuing the rule once the battles were won.

The invention of the Machine-Tractor Stations (MTS) owned by the state had preceded forced collectivization, and this institution solved the problem of how to bring party rule to rural USSR. According to Leninist principle, party discipline depends upon keeping membership to a relatively small select group. In the early 1930s the Party could not attempt to control some quarter of a million collectives by manning them with primary party units of a score or so comrades on each farm. However, the MTS numbered only a few thousand; the Party could, and did, afford the manpower to create strong political units within them,[11] and the monopoly they were given over the farms' major equipment provided the lever to control agricultural production.

THE STALINIST KOLKHOZY

Many important changes have occurred in the USSR since Stalin's death in 1953. Among the more important innovations in agriculture, we should point out that peasant incomes have been improved. The MTS were abandoned by Khrushchev because they had become an expensive, no longer necessary, arm of control over the villages. So many farms were amalgamated in the early 1950s that the already large collectives were transformed into huge leviathans. Yet today's *kolkhoz* (collective) and *sovkhoz* (state) farms remain basically the same rural institutions evolved under Stalin. True, there has been a move to provide the *kolkhoz* members with a guaranteed annual wage, whereas in Stalin's day the major difference in practice between the two types of farm was that the *sovkhoz* worker had a guaranteed state wage, while the *kolkhoz* member's income depended upon the success of the farm from year to year. Yet when seen from the view of the peasants working directly with the crops and livestock, the difference between the two organizational forms must have seemed small. Then and now the average Soviet peasant must regard himself as a rural labourer who has little or no influence over the operation of the farm he lives on.

Theoretically each *kolkhoz* is under the control of a general meeting of all the members as 'the highest authority' on the farm. On paper the Model Charter of Agricultural Artels, adopted in 1935, is a 'basic law' that provides for a highly democratic organization of rural life. In practice, however, the 'democratically' elected farm chairmen are appointed from above as are the directors of the *sovkhozy*, and their appointment is later rubber-stamped by a vote in a general meeting. Indeed, through the institution of the *nomenklature* ('appointments list') the nomination of new chairmen must have the approval of regional or higher party authorities.

Each farm is divided into several production and service branches which vary according to its particular production needs. There are field crop units, vegetable raising and animal husbandry branches, and such subsidiary activities as carpenters' shops and machine repair sheds. Most of the work is organized through large livestock and field working brigades (often numbering over 100 workers), headed by brigade leaders who, along with their immediate assistants, comprise the lowest rank of the managerial personnel on the farms. In spite of the repeated boast that Soviet agriculture is highly mechanized, when contrasted with most Western systems a surprising amount of the work is still done with simple hand implements.

Along with the chairman, other key farm managers – e.g. the chief agronomist, chief accountant, and managers of livestock and field sections – comprise the *kolkhoz* administration which, according to the Model Charter, is to carry out policy decisions made in the periodic general meetings of the membership. In practice, however, Soviet literature reveals that the general meetings have been very infrequent and with rare exception (especially during the Second World War, a period of relatively relaxed controls over the countryside), they serve only to rubber-stamp decisions made by the administration. Indeed, since the amalgamations of the early 1950s, the average farm is so large that general meetings of the whole membership are nearly impossible. Thus many, if not most, farms have evolved a representation system to reduce attendance at such gatherings. Clearly, on-the-farm decisions are in the hands of the chairman and his staff. When I visited rural Russia in 1960, I came away with the impression that the *kolkhoz* chairman must be held in nearly as much awe by the ordinary peasant member as were the former Tsarist landlords (or their farm managers) before the Revolution. In spite of the so-called democracy of the general meeting, the real political nature of the *kolkhozy* is perhaps best expressed in the Article of the Model Charter that charges the chairmen even to enter the peasants' homes to include the women in the system, not merely as additional field hands, but as members of the social fabric of the collective as well.

Unfortunately for work efficiency, the chairman and the other members of the collective's administration are not after all as powerful as they might seem to the ordinary peasant. Until Khrushchev abandoned the MTS in 1958, the monopoly of these state agencies over major farm equipment allowed such non-farm officials as the MTS tractor brigade leaders, MTS directors and MTS chief agronomists to make many of the important production decisions for the farms they serviced. Most important of all were the staffs of MTS party inspectors who were held individually responsible for the success of specific farms. Such above-the-farm party inspectors still exist, attached to district offices now that the MTS have been disbanded and their machines sold to the farms.

Polish and Yugoslavian state farms have their workers' councils and the collective *ejido* of Mexico have similar groups, and, as noted, the *kolkhozy* theoretically operate under '*kolkhoz* democracy'. Unfortunately, both the literature and personal observation in all of these systems will document a conclusion that such institutions can give the average peasant little sense of participation in the operation of the farm, beyond that of a hired hand receiving orders. This reality is at the heart of the costly losses in food production that characterize such systems. No wonder, therefore, that the small private family garden plots and the few animals Stalin allowed the peasant families to retain when he forced them into the collectives have received the peasants' major attention, at the expense of collective production. Moreover, from the beginning, quite out of proportion to the size of these tiny plots, that average less than an acre, a significant portion of the peasants' income and the nation's food have come from this source.

KUKURUZA AND PERSONALITY

Other than the amalgamation of the *kolkhozy* into ever huger farms, from the early 1930s until 1958 no major change occurred in the system of ruling the countryside. During the Second World War Moscow apparently encouraged the rumour that a relaxation of controls over the farms would follow victory. However, one of the first major post-war programmes was designed to recapture the parcels of *kolkhozy* land that the peasants had added to their private plots during the relaxed conditions of the war. Stalin retained his monopoly of power until 1953, yet, strangely, with his famed *agrogorod* scheme of urbanizing the villages Khrushchev captured the leadership in agriculture three years before Stalin's death.

Khrushchev's vision of the *agro* (agricultural) *gorod* (city, shortened to *grad* in names such as Stalingrad or Leningrad) was hardly original. The eventual elimination of differences between cities and villages is part of the promised achievement of full communism. What was new in 1950 was that early in that year Khrushchev set forth proposals that seemed to call for an immediate reconstruction of the countryside into rural cities with good dwellings, schools, hospitals, film theatres, libraries and all the rest of the cultural amenities enjoyed by city dwellers. Hopefully, the future will reveal whether or not in promoting the building of cities on the farms Khrushchev really believed for a short while that the Soviet economy could afford the enormous cost of rebuilding the countryside. Such a transformation would have taken at least a decade, and the price would have put an end to rapid industrial growth. Whatever his long-range plans, his scheme silenced fellow Politburo member Andreyev's suggestion that the *zveno* (link) example should be universally followed. During and after the war some farms had abandoned the large brigade system of organizing the work, and instead had virtually divided themselves into small independent production units of a few hundred hectares for which *zveno*, groups of half a dozen or so individuals, were responsible. According to Andreyev, farms which had created *zveno* were producing significantly more than the large farms where the work was still organized in brigades. Nevertheless, Khrushchev (with the aid of Stalin) silenced the pro-*zveno* forces, and they were not to be heard from again until the 1960s (see Chapter 6 below).[12]

Whatever Khrushchev's real intention, amalgamating the already large collectives into even larger units seemed to be the necessary first step towards creating the *agrogorods*, and before it became clear that the rural cities were not to be built, a nationwide drive to unify the 'smaller farms' was well under way. By 1958 the average farm was several times larger than it had been in 1949, and the total number of *kolkhozy* was reduced from some 240,000 to less than 70,000 – and to 36,300 by 1966.[13] Whereas the Party could not have afforded to staff the quarter of a million smaller farms, by 1958 virtually every farm had a party member chairman and a party unit. In a single drive in the early 1950s, 20,000 comrades were dispatched from the cities to offer themselves as candidates for posts as farm chairmen. As a result the MTS became redundant, and in a single speech Khrushchev sent them on their way to oblivion.[14]

Stalin's 'revolution from above' had captured control over the farms through the MTS outposts, but as long as the party presence remained outside the farms, the link between the peasants and Moscow remained indirect. It was Khrushchev's amalgamations that welded the final link in the bureaucratic chain of command that was essential to Stalin's system of rule in the cities. Prior to 1958 only the *sovkhozy* offered, besides a guaranteed wage, direct on-the-farm party leadership. After 1958, although the *kolkhoz* peasants were yet to receive a guarantee of a stable income, they too joined the single hierarchy of rewards and punishments that now encompassed the whole of society. 1958 also saw the beginning of a new era of 'mature' totalitarian rule, in which the Stalinist use of terror as a key instrument of power had been abandoned. It was, however still true that 'the ruling philosophy that guides the regime embodies an attempt to encompass every facet of human existence, and ... has in fact, achieved a notable level of success in enmeshing ... all its citizens in a single bureaucratic web'.[15] With the Party fully entrenched on the farms, the promise of the 1917 revolution to socialize the entire society was now fulfilled.

Although neither of them abandoned the slogan of 'all [economic] priority to industrial construction', Stalin and especially Khrushchev showed serious concern over the need to increase food and fibre production. Stalin stayed in Moscow, created commissions, and published an occasional tract. Khrushchev, however, built his career on promises to solve agriculture's problems by such schemes as amalgamation, corn growing and new lands campaigns, and by offering the inspiration of his personality in hundreds of speeches delivered on tours that crisscrossed the countryside numerous times. His faith in corn (maize) as the 'queen of the fields', which earned him the nickname of 'Kukuruznik' (Corn-chap), meant that, for a time, corn was widely planted in areas quite unsuited for the crop. In the mid 1950s he implied that harvests from the once 'virgin lands' of the arid regions of Southern Russia and Kazakhstan would solve the grain problem, and under his guidance millions of new hectares were put to the plough. Dust storms were the result, and much less of the area is now under cultivation. Such were the economic aspects of his policy, but a complete catalogue of his efforts will reveal that he inherited from Stalin a conviction that the major key to agricultural success lay in the political realm of finding the correct managerial scheme for the farms. Amalgamating the collectives, promoting the superiority of the *sovkhoz* administrative form, bringing city party 'volunteers' to the farms as chairmen, changing about ministries and agencies in Moscow, abandoning the MTS, and his final major act of erecting the Territorial Production Administrations as a new local agency, Party-directed, ruling over several farms and designed to recapture some of the MTS advantages, were all primarily political moves. They were accompanied by volumes of words that might have been summarized as follows. 'The *kolkhozy* and *sovkhozy* are the world's most advanced form of agricultural organization. These farms provide the prototype of the huge industrial farms of the future. At present the relationships between the farms and Moscow need improvement. Similarly the internal production organization of the farms needs strengthening. Nevertheless, the correct formulas for collectivized administration will be discovered in the near future, and when they are, our farms will prove to be the most efficient agricultural units in the world.' Indeed, as each new administrative reform was announced, Khrushchev heralded it as providing the final breakthrough. Unfortunately, each in turn proved to be only a tinkering with the machinery that had little or no positive effect.

The new leadership which took over in the fall of 1964 has still to complete its record in agriculture. Some needed changes are in the making; nevertheless, as the 1970 decade dawns, indications are that politics as usual continue to dominate the countryside. The huge collective and state farms which combine local government functions with the production function seem destined to persist. The central leadership still seems to feel the need to exact maximum political controls over agriculture, which are ideally provided by the *kolkhoz–sovkhoz* system. The story of collectivized agricultural politics is not complete, however, without a review of the beliefs that evolved in support of the *kolkhozy* and *sovkhozy*.

CHAPTER 3

Collectivization: the Strength of the Myth*

To be successful, even just to survive in office, political leaders everywhere must be pragmatic. Even in the USSR, where the leadership is deeply committed to the ideology of communism, an examination of policy making will reveal important practical demands behind each policy change. This is as true in agriculture as it is in other realms of Soviet affairs. Yet, having recognized this, we must also credit Marxist–Leninist thought with having an enormous influence over Soviet agricultural policy. Not only has communist ideology provided the vocabulary Soviet leaders use in describing farm policy, but the emotional investment in their agricultural system, aside from the immense economic investment, is so deep that to repudiate the huge collective and state farms surely would result in an enormous loss of pride, for it would also mean repudiating their claim that their politico–economic experiment has an important contribution to make to rural organization elsewhere in the world.

Although Soviet beliefs about agriculture have been modified over the years, the basic Marxist–Leninist tenets remain, and without some grasp of the evolved doctrine the Western observer is often at a loss to understand the choices selected in making new agricultural policy. These are part of a society's total myth system, 'the value-impregnated beliefs and notions

*Most of the material presented in this chapter is an amalgam of two studies of Soviet beliefs already published. See Roy D. Laird, 'Collectivization: New and Old Myths', *Studies of the Soviet Union*, vol. VI, No. 4, 1967, pp. 78–88, and 'The New Soviet Myth: Marx is Dead, Long Live Communism!', *Soviet Studies*, vol. XVII, No. 4, April 1967, pp. 511–18.

that men hold, that they live by or live for'.[1] In the USSR these beliefs are part of the constantly changing corpus of communist ideology.

Professor Alfred G. Meyer, the author of the brilliant study *Leninism*, has written, 'the leaders of the Communist Party really do believe in communism as they understand it'. Nevertheless, he continues, 'are they really communists? I am not sure whether it should even be asked.'[2] If the test for being a communist measures one's slavish adherence to quasi-religious doctrine, as might be the test for many communicants of more conventional religions, Soviet evidence would tend to reinforce the doubt Professor Meyer's question raises. Indeed, as nearly as one can be sure of such judgements, Soviet agricultural policies have often been in defiance of doctrine, responding instead to pressing political and economic needs, as was Lenin's adoption of the New Economic Policy in 1921. Therefore, much of the staying power of the Soviet system must be credited to the leaders' ability to invent new, seemingly communist myths in the face of pressing demands of the moment. Yet, is not a major test of belief the demonstrated need to argue, no matter how far-fetched the rationalization, that a new policy really squares with the long-professed dogma? No matter how tortuous the task has been, the Soviet leadership has always invented some explanation that sounds consistent with Marxism–Leninism for new policies that, to the Western observer, obviously are but responses to pragmatic needs.

We should not, however, impose a standard of rigid adherence to doctrine upon the communist that has not been observable in other belief systems. All such systems exhibit a conflict between change and resistance to change, which through compromise reluctantly grants a partial victory to the changers. As a result, all the great religions of the world have evolved and are evolving into belief systems quite different from those established by their original leaders. Seen in this light, the myths about rural society and production discussed below are best described as elements of an evolving belief system which have sprung from both Marxist–Leninist doctrine and pragmatic responses to economic and political needs. The Soviet leaders are not only communists but, like all men, believing animals, and so any explanation of post-1917 policies in rural Russia based solely upon the narrowly political (e.g., power-oriented) and economic factors would be both sterile and misleading. Hobbes and Marx were right: seeking one power after another and making responses to economic imperatives are vital determinants of political behaviour, but so is man's need to quiet his conscience by conforming his actions to some view of the good and the true. Communism provided the basis for the emerging Soviet belief system. Marxist–Leninist descriptions of the right way do more than just determine the leadership's explanation of what they have done. Communist texts also provide the word picture of much of what 'they live by or live for'.

MARX AND THE MIR

Although he claimed to approach human affairs from a universal base, Karl Marx's view that economic need determines all human activity, and that the impact of the industrial revolution on the economic environment provided the key to all future change, was highly parochial and futuristic, blind to the immediate wants and needs of the bulk of mankind. His theories were built upon observations of the forces at work in urbanizing and industrializing Western Europe and North America, while he largely ignored that great bulk of the world's population that in the middle of the last century lived in rural areas of the globe, practically untouched by industrial change. Surely, one of the greatest ironies of modern history is that revolutions inspired by Marxism–Leninism have succeeded only in predominantly peasant and agricultural societies.

With one curious exception, what little attention Marx and Engels devoted to rural problems rested upon the assumption that urban economic change would sweep the peasantry into the mainstream of the industrial revolution. In line with Engels's view in *Anti-Dühring* that in the original state of nature, man had held land in common, perhaps a communal (*obshchina*) seed of socialism had been preserved in the *mir* (the village commune). Perhaps, a primitive socialist consciousness fostered by the *mir* could provide an important spark for a communist revolution in Russia.[3] Marx's impact on agricultural thought, however, was based almost entirely upon his belief in the universal application of the industrial method of production. Therefore, his major contribution to the agricultural myth system was the conviction that, as in the case of industry, agriculture too was destined to be concentrated in fewer and fewer hands, agricultural production too would become highly mechanized, and agriculture too would adopt the managerial patterns that had been evolved in industry. In short, large scale industrialized farming would prove to be the most efficient form of food production which, in time, would dissolve the differences between urban and rural societies.

LENIN v. STALIN

Marx's argument that only nationalization would allow the proper equal relation of all members of society to the means of production was the political key to organizing society correctly. In agriculture, therefore, nationalization of the land was explicit in the Marxian 'science', and some sort of collective or state organization and management of the large industrial farming units was implicit. Faced with the responsibility of leading a state created in the name of Marxist communism, Lenin was left with the detail of putting the theory into practice. The lessons of the 1905 rehearsal of the 1917 revolution had provided Lenin with insights that led to success in

1917, lessons which were embodied in his two major revisions of the doctrine. First of all the Party had to be transformed into a highly disciplined vanguard that would provide a political elite capable of leading a successful revolution, and, since the peasantry comprised the great bulk of Russian society, success could be achieved only if the Party vanguard could effectively harness the forces for agrarian revolution.

In Lenin's eyes, although the peasants were less class-conscious than the urban proletariat, the middle and especially the well-to-do (*kulak*) peasantry were seen as hopelessly bourgeois. However, the great bulk of the peasants who were landless, or short of land, were seen as being in a position in relation to the rural means of production that was socially and psychologically analagous to the position of the exploited urban wage-slave. Thus in 1908 Lenin nominated that bulk of Russia's rural masses who were desperately poor into a 'semi-proletarian' class. In his view, the growing 'Russian agrarian crisis . . . [is] taking place in conditions in which the peasantry is being transformed into a rural bourgeoisie and a prole-tariat . . .'[4]

Building upon this sort of thinking, Lenin reduced the slogan of the 1917 revolution to a peasant-oriented phrase, 'Peace, land, and bread.' Not only did he come to recognize that the success of the revolution depended upon the alliance that he had helped to build with the poor peasants, but also he believed that the future survival of Bolshevik rule depended upon concessions to peasant demands. In the long haul, however, agriculture must be industrialized (hence his dictum, 'communism is the Soviet power plus the electrification of the whole country'), which in practice meant some form of collectivization. Indeed, for Lenin the need to 'adopt large scale, collective and mechanized agriculture' amounted to an 'indisputable theoretical truth'.[5] However, non-proletarian rural habits were so deeply ingrained in most of the peasants that if they were pushed too fast, the results could be disastrous.

In short, Lenin believed that communist construction in the countryside must be 'gradual', built brick by brick upon peasants' voluntary acceptance of the superiority of communist production forms. More than once he warned that it 'would be absolutely absurd to attempt to reshape these [millions of individual] farms in any rapid way'. Again, the 'state must effect the transition to collective farming with extreme caution and only very gradually, by the force of example, without any coercion of [even] the middle peasant'.[6]

Stalin, of course, abandoned Lenin's strictures against forced collectivization. Perhaps the crux of Stalin's disagreement with Leninist dogma was Lenin's undying belief that the Russian revolution was primarily the staging ground for the imminent proletarian revolution in industrialized Europe. One can reasonably argue that had Lenin lived for a number of years beyond 1924, he, like Stalin, would have broken with the dream of the European revolution and turned full efforts to creating socialism in one country. Once the Soviet leadership did this, collectivization offered far more than just the promise of bringing communism to the Russian countryside. Whatever Lenin might have done, Stalin turned all his thoughts and efforts to internal construction, and in his eagerness to establish heavy industry as quickly as possible, set about forcing the peasants into the collectives, thus creating institutions that would permit maximum controls over the countryside, and from which could be extracted the capital needed for industry.

While Stalin's concern with what he saw as the pragmatic demands of industrial construction upon agriculture primarily determined his agricultural policies, he obviously believed collective farms were superior institutions and apparently persuaded himself that most of the poor peasants joined the collectivization drive voluntarily – 'the overwhelming bulk of the peasantry simply join[ed] the collective farms'.[7] The Western critic may rightly disbelieve this judgement. Nevertheless many poor peasants eagerly joined the 'committees of the poor', first organized by Lenin and successfully resurrected to defeat general peasant opposition to the collectives. Therefore there was at least a core of rural 'proletariat' whom Stalin believed to be capable of leading the struggle for higher production achievements, once the proper organizational form had been created.

Although the timing of Stalin's rural policy actions was dictated largely by his view of industry's needs, the literature of the time repeatedly expressed the belief that collectivization had allowed the countryside to join the march to communism. He could hardly have declared the arrival of socialism in one state in 1936 if collectivization had not been achieved. Moreover, a new doctrine was proclaimed: the collective and state farms would prove to be so much more efficient than the old ways of organizing production that soon the whole of rural society would enthusiastically support them. Continued increase in the size of the farms reflected a conviction that the larger the farm, the greater the potential for efficient production. Stalinist literature also expressed the belief that the *sovkhozy* were a higher form of production than the *kolkhozy*, and that a marriage of the Marxist–Leninist 'science' and natural science would ultimately allow the transformation of nature to a point where agriculture would enjoy the same controlled conditions of production that had been achieved in much of industry. Furthermore, the chief party biologist Lysenko managed to incorporate Marxism–Leninism in his 'genetics' (actually, he rejected the gene theory), promising increased production with a minimum of investment, and thereby secured the favour of Stalin and the leadership of Soviet agricultural science.

KHRUSHCHEV AND HIS SUCCESSORS

Stalin's successors may well wonder at times whether Lenin's voluntary path would not have been better than the Stalinist road of force. Nevertheless, the collective and state farms that exist are part of the heritage that must be believed in, and there is no evidence that the post-1953 leadership has rejected the myth of the superiority of large-scale collectivized agriculture – after all, they combine the communist and industrial organizational forms. Clearly, however, the new leadership believes that the system can be improved upon. Stalin saw little need for change in the system during his time. He stoutly rejected the suggestion that the *zveno* might be superior to the huge brigades as the basic means of organizing the work on the farms. Even the state-owned MTS were proclaimed to be sacrosanct, long after the growth of the party's presence on the farm meant that the MTS control over the machinery was no longer needed to assure control over the peasantry. Stalin firmly rejected the suggestion that the MTS machinery be sold to the collectives, for such an act would involve 'a step in reversion to the old backwardness . . . trying to turn back the wheel of history'.[8]

In contrast to Stalin's conservatism, the almost frantic attempts of Khrushchev and his successors at various administrative reforms have once again revealed a belief that when organizational relationships in rural Russia can be set right, the key will be found to increasing production. The MTS were dismantled under Khrushchev, and even the heretical idea of the *zveno* was discussed and briefly experimented with. Certainly, although construction of heavy industry is still said to receive first priority in investment, the significant increases in agricultural investment represent an important change from the old myth of 'all priority to industry'. While Stalin in his valedictory work, *Economic Problems of Socialism in the USSR*, expressed a concern that the dragging feet of agriculture were holding back industrial progress, he did nothing about the problem. Now there seems to be a new belief that many more roubles than ever before must be poured into agriculture if a serious slow-down in the growth of the economy is to be prevented. A measure of this change in attitude was given in Brezhnev's observation that the projected investment in agriculture for the five-year period ending in 1970 is 'approximately as much as the investment in agriculture during the nineteen years following the war'.[9]

Part of the investment is to go into new investigations into science and its application to increased production. The number of trained specialists working on the farms started to increase significantly under Khrushchev and continued under Brezhnev and Kosygin. Whereas under Stalin very few trained specialists lived on the farms, by 'April 1, 1965, 40·7 per cent of the engineers and technicians in the *kolkhozy*, 67·3 per cent of the *kolkhoz* chairmen, 10·1 per cent of the production brigade leaders and 10·8 per cent of the heads of livestock sections had university or secondary specialized education'.[10] Obviously, the leadership believes that the impact of such a managerial revolution on the farms will be beneficial.

THE COMMITMENT TO COLLECTIVIZATION: 1960S AND BEYOND

To paraphrase the great American humourist Will Rogers, the student of Soviet affairs knows only what he reads in the Soviet newspapers. The intelligent reader must read also between the lines, whether of *Pravda* or the *New York Times*, because the private thoughts of leaders often differ significantly from their published utterances. Yet those who once thought Soviet statistics were often doctored for Western consumption found no significant discrepancies between what had been published in the Stalinist press and what was contained in secret economic documents that fell into German hands, to be liberated by

Western armies, during the Second World War. The invention of the big lie is credited to Hitler, yet he had published the truth in his *Mein Kampf*. Undoubtedly, the Soviet leadership entertains private thoughts about collectivization and its future. Undoubtedly, pressing pragmatic demands will dictate the adoption of what seem to be un-communist policies in Western eyes. Yet reading both on the lines and between the lines leaves one with the impression of a substantial collectivization myth, not the least part of which is the firm belief that, however reorganized in the future, the collectivized system is destined to continue, because it is the best possible means of organizing the countryside. After Khrushchev, necessity gave a new lease of life to the peasants' private plots, which may provide as much as a third of the nation's food. Yet no doubt is left that at some future date this malignancy must be cut out of the collectivized system.

The Soviet leadership is constantly concerned about the education and propagandization of the citizenry, and the *kolkhozy* are repeatedly credited with being valuable schools of communism. Under Stalin, only a small number of the farms afforded party units, but by 1 January 1965 the average *kolkhoz* boasted a party unit of some forty members.[11] The central leadership's faith in the new party presence on the farms, enforced by increased specialized training among the cadres, may mean that the long-admitted need for greater decentralization in production decision-making can now be satisfied. Perhaps, though, a long history of unfulfilled promises, coupled with Minister of Agriculture V. V. Matskevich's emphatic assignment of responsibility for farm 'operational direction' to local (*raion*) or regional (*oblast* or *krai*) and republic administrations, in order to guarantee fulfilment of state purchase plans, points in the old direction.[12] Since the authoritarian leadership system still believes in the need for tight central controls, and since new sociological evidence has been produced to substantiate the long-held and little-disguised belief in the social inferiority of the peasantry, it is probable that the Soviet leadership will continue using the *kolkhozy* to keep a tight rein on a backward peasantry.

In a most revealing study of peasant attitudes, quite unusual for Soviet social science, Russian Republic statistics for 1961 are cited to indicate that the *kolkhoz* peasant's income from his private plot averaged 628 roubles, and a *sovkhoz* worker's 465 roubles. Assertedly, 'the closer the private plot brings the *kolkhoz* peasant to the [urban] workers materially in level of income, the more strongly they are separated from the workers in the social respect'. Again, in the study of a representative farming area, whereas only 7 per cent of rural homes where heads of families are engaged in skilled work had icons, 57 per cent of the homes of the unskilled peasants had icons.[13] Now modern social science findings can be cited to substantiate Lenin's belief in the lagging 'semi-proletarian' social consciousness of the peasantry.

Of course, it is now believed that significant progress has been made in altering the social consciousness of the peasantry, that the differences that exist between the cities and the farms are gradually disappearing. Similarly, the major differences between the 'two forms of property', the *kolkhozy* and *sovkhozy*, are said almost to have vanished. Realization of the promise of a guaranteed *kolkhoz* wage, increased investments in the *kolkhozy*, and the increasing parity of esteem for mental and physical labour, plus other changes, are said to be 'overcoming the socio-economic and cultural distinctions between the town and the country',[14] and between the *kolkhozy* and *sovkhozy*. Although the post-Stalin press has emphasized repeatedly that the *kolkhozy* and *sovkhozy* are to be regarded as virtually equal on the ladder of socialist development, a hint of a belief in the slight superiority of the *sovkhozy* persists. Indeed, while arguing that the socialist development of the *kolkhozy* and *sovkhozy* is virtually the same, a *kolkhoz* chairman admits that there is a 'theoretical basis for turning weak *kolkhozy* into *sovkhozy*'.[15]

The dream fashioned from an amalgam of the Russian feeling for the limitless steppes and the Marxist–Leninist faith in the superiority of large-scale industrialized agriculture has not faded. The continued amalgamation of the already huge farms into even larger ones continues. The long-held tendency to believe that hugeness and production efficiency are twins was carried to the extreme under Khrushchev, and under his aegis the size of the average collective increased by more than four-fold between 1950 and 1964. After Khrushchev's fall, Brezhnev's first remarks implied a recognition that giganto-mania had got out of hand, that amalgamation had been carried to extremes. 'Some *kolkhozy* became so huge that they proved to be unmanageable.'[16] Similarly, the process in recent years of changing over many of the collectives to *sovkhozy* was said to have gone too far. Yet neither trend has been reversed. Indeed, 1965 showed a still further increase in the size of the farms from 1964, the number of *kolkhozy* dropping from some 38,300 to 36,900, while the number of *sovkhozy* increased from 10,078 to 11,642.[17] If this process does not stop soon the whole of the countryside will be one huge *sovkhoz*. Perhaps the future may see some of the farms divided, but published Soviet studies on the optimum size of the farms reiterate faith in the present large units. One manifestation of the gigantomania theme, however, does seem to have been modified: Khrush-chev's vast new lands programme is no longer advertised as the answer to the need for increased production. His successors seem to have concluded that the key to greater food output lies in increasing yields in established areas, and there is therefore considerable emphasis on a new land improvement programme that 'should embrace all areas of the country, every collective and state farm'.[18]

The lie that the bulk of the peasants originally entered the collectives voluntarily is still repeated. Perhaps it will eventually be repudiated. Yet the belief that most collectives are democratically managed, and that all can and should be so managed, is stoutly defended. Thus, for example, a *kolkhoz* chairman has insisted that every *kolkhoz* member must actively participate in managing the affairs of the public farm.[19] In a reverse sort of way, the continued dramatization by the press of the evils present on farms that fail to live up to the democratic ideal is proof of the importance of this exercise in self-delusion. Those who might doubt the strength of this conviction should perhaps be reminded of the millions of Americans who long expressed a passionate belief in the near perfection of American democracy, in seeming ignorance of the second-class status of the black and brown portions of the population. The great importance of the myth of *kolkhoz* democracy is further testified by President Podgorny's reference at the Twenty-third Party Congress to what must be done in drafting new Rules of the Agricultural Artels, when he concentrated nearly all his remarks upon the observation that the document would provide an 'improvement in the democratic methods of managing *kolkhoz* life'.[20]

The myths of a society are fashioned not only from the obvious environment (*vide* Marx's famous dictum, 'life is not determined by consciousness, but consciousness by life'), but much more subtly by those parts of the environment which the leadership and the members of the society select as important. As suggested previously, the changing myths of Soviet collectivization are rooted both in Marxist–Leninist doctrine and the lessons of experience. However come by, they seem to be deeply entrenched after more than a quarter century of the existence of the farms. Of course, the desire for economic and political control over the peasants has become part of the myth, but beyond these needs are less tangible, more purely ideological supports for the continued strength of collectivization.

Collectivization fits the ideology's demand for bringing communism to the countryside for at least three reasons. First of all, it serves to equalize peasant society. Secondly, and most importantly, the *kolkhozy* and *sovkhozy* are seen as the correct media for industrializing agriculture, however mistaken and costly this aim may be. And thirdly, the farms satisfy a penchant for hugeness. The size of the farms and of the work brigades can be explained up to a point by the need for maximum control, but particularly in face of evidence that the small *zveno* work units are much more efficient, there is hardly any compelling economic argument that the present system of huge brigades is the most desirable form of organizing the work; it seems to spring from a faith – rooted both in Marxian and traditional Russian beliefs – in size for its own sake.

Perhaps the most important of all the myths that make collectivization attractive is that fashioned from a wedding of Marxist–Leninist 'science' with scientism, that is, the widespread hope that just as natural scientists have used their mathematical disciplines to build super weapons and to produce wonder drugs, so the same precise techniques can be employed to solve the major problems of human relations. Since communism is dominated by a faith in material and human perfectibility, collectivization seems to promise the best way to organize the transformation of nature in search of the promised heaven on earth.

The farms now constitute an emotional investment of more than a quarter century; if the system were abandoned, such an act would amount to an unprecedented admission of grave error on the part of the Party. After all, can Soviet society be expected to abandon the collectivization prescribed by Marxism–Leninism when, in but a half century, backward Tsarist Russia has been transformed into the world's second major power, all in the name of the ideology? Moreover, with all the serious failings in the system and the inhuman sacrifices imposed by Stalin, the lot of the individual peasant has improved. And it must not be forgotten that, ironically, in spite of wide advertisement of the inefficiency of the Soviet agricultural system, the collectives represent a living model for organizing the peasantry in other developing countries. To abandon collectivization would be to undercut the communists' most important argument for persuading native national liberation movements in predominantly peasant developing nations to accept the Soviet lead. It is no surprise that the myths that have grown up about Soviet agriculture strongly support the collective farms. Unfortunately, fundamental changes in the system that would seriously challenge these beliefs are needed if Soviet agriculture is to solve its very grave problems.

Part Two

THE POTENTIAL
OF COLLECTIVIZATION

CHAPTER 4

Science and Soviet Agriculture

SCIENCE has been proclaimed by Soviet leaders as containing the answers to all man's problems. Communism itself is considered a scientific approach to human existence. Science has, of course, contributed vastly to man's range of knowledge and, in fact, has made possible most modern advances in agriculture. But what is the current role of agricultural science in the Soviet Union? After periodic setbacks, can we not expect Soviet science to forge ahead and provide the knowledge which will in turn significantly increase production? What are the trends in agricultural biology and chemistry and in the burgeoning social sciences where they touch on rural society?

Science, of course, is the search for new knowledge through the establishment of verifiable principles, which are arrived at by employing the long-established methodology of setting up hypotheses and accepting or rejecting them after carrying out testing procedures, procedures which can be repeated by any capable investigator who wishes to verify any new principles which may be claimed. Rigid adherence to methodology is a key to the achievements of the chemist in the laboratory, the agricultural geneticist in the field plot, and the social scientist in an interview, using a standardized questionnaire.

1964: KHRUSHCHEV, THE CULT AND LYSENKOISM

The world-wide explosion of scientific knowledge has been so enormous that in order to expand knowledge still further, most contemporary scientists require rather expensive backing to support the purchase of equipment, pay the salaries of research assistants, etc. As a result, few new discoveries are made any longer by the isolated investigator in his private laboratory, once a self-equipped work room in the back of his home. This change is of vital importance since the present environment for new discovery demands sustained and ever more substantial economic support from public or private financial sources. In turn, such support is dependent upon a society's willingness to finance scientific investigation, which is not, in practice, easily aroused. Thus, although long before 1957 the American public had seemed to agree that most new social and economic advances stem from scientific research, it was the shock of the first Sputnik launching in the fall of 1957 that prompted the United States government's decision to provide a whole new level of public financial support for education and research.

There now seems to be a new Soviet attitude towards science in agriculture. In this case the shock that precipitated the change was probably the serious harvest failure of 1963 which followed the slowing down in food output after the 1958-9 peak, and which forced the painful decision to purchase huge quantities of grain from abroad, including from the United States. Khrushchev's period of rule had provided an important and long-needed relaxation of restrictions on Soviet life. Ironically, however, although he concentrated most of his attention to internal problems on the dire needs of agriculture, the basic pattern of politics which had been so damaging to agriculture and agriculture-related science in the past was little improved. Indeed, Khrushchev accompanied his exaggerated promises for his various production campaigns with repeated advertising of Lysenko's asserted scientific findings at Lenin Hills, thereby permitting Lysenko to reach a new peak of dominance over agricultural biology.

Most of the sorry Lysenko record has been widely publicized. However, two related points need to be made. First of all, although Lysenkoism (defined as the view that acquired characteristics can be transmitted from one generation to the next) seemed to reach a new height of popularity under Khrushchev, on balance, the situation in the biological and agricultural sciences probably improved under his relatively liberal leadership. For example, a colleague at the University of Kansas, a geneticist who visited a number of Soviet laboratories in the early 1960s, noted that away from the research centres dominated by the 'Lysenkoist frauds', he met a substantial number of solid biological scientists. Secondly, however, the term Lysenkoism might also be used to describe an ideologically imposed attitude that has had its impact on all Soviet science, that is, a belief that 'Marxist–Leninist science' provides an advanced base for all science, thereby allowing the achievement of a level of discovery unobtainable in pre-communist settings. In this case Khrushchev's apparent utter confidence in his own schemes and campaigns might be seen as Lysenkoist, representing a special Marxist–Leninist approach to science and innovation.

Much of what was specifically wrong in agriculture-related science in the early 1960s has been subsequently catalogued by Soviet writers, leaders, and the scientists themselves. These criticisms were related primarily to problems of investment, education, dissemination of knowledge to the farms, and standards of work.

Investment in scientific investigation even now, but particularly as it was prior to 1964, is criticized as being much too low.[1] As a result, although no exact figures seem to have been published, a significant part of the 41 billion roubles to be spent on agriculture during the 1966–70 five-year plan was designated for research and its application. The number of specialized research institutions was to be increased.[2] Since the new leadership decided that future production increases must come primarily from increased yields in established agricultural areas, a vast land improvement programme has been initiated, and the USSR Ministry of Land Reclamation and Water Resources created for this purpose is to have its own research facilities.[3] A further criticism has been voiced, that a comprehensive soil mapping programme is long overdue.[4]

Education and training in agricultural science is now particularly stressed. Apparently there have not been enough young people of quality in the recent training programmes.[5] A scientific-age problem, familiar in Western universities, is said to exist. Many of the top professors have been criticized for spending full time in their laboratories, and failing to lecture and guide their students.[6] New programmes and new stress on science education in agriculture seem to be in the making.

Dissemination of new knowledge to the farms appears to be even more difficult in the USSR than it is in the more developed nations. There are far too few outlets for the publication of results by young researchers,[7] and the complaint is heard that some research establishments have no outlets for publishing the findings even of their senior staff.[8] The time gap between discovery and practical application is said to be therefore discouragingly large. Great concern over the problem has been expressed, and Premier Kosygin has called for a new system of disseminating scientific information.[9]

Standards in agricultural science are said to be far too low. Indeed, this seems to be the most crucial problem of all. Some research centres are accused of having lowered their standards even below those of the Khrushchev era.[10] Undesirable attitudes carried over from the past are apparently the prime cause for a situation in which not enough qualified trainees are entering the profession.[11] Rather than being left alone to pursue their research, scientists have been pressured to waste their efforts on production activities.[12] Under both Stalin and Khrushchev, the social science side of agricultural production problems was left almost totally unexplored. Thus the study of rural attitudes cited in the previous chapter represents a landmark in the advance of Soviet social science.[13] Most important of all, however, the Lysenkoist climate is now openly admitted to have wrought 'enormous' harm to agricultural science.[14] Clear admission is made that, under Khrushchev, researchers were able to impose the application of their supposed discoveries upon the farms without tests being made of their scientific validity.

THE NEW ENVIRONMENT v. LEADERSHIP CHARACTERISTICS

The new leadership's admission that 'urgent measures' must be taken in agriculture precipitated not only the decision greatly to increase investment in agriculture, but also a resolve to alter the climate in which the agricultural scientist must work. Thus, the Twenty-third Party Congress directive 'to raise the responsibility of research institutions for the scientific substantiation of their findings' is being stressed.[15] Indeed, Lysenko's operation at Lenin Hills was reviewed by a team of investigators from key academies which 'confirmed that the factual material that T. D. Lysenko published in the press is not true'.[16] As a result, Lysenkoism as a party-backed genetic theory is finished, and Soviet biology appears to have entered a new and more promising era. However, as implied earlier, Lysenkoism grew out of a particular atmosphere involving a special Marxist–Leninist approach to science and innovation, an atmosphere that feeds dogmatism and encourages over-optimism, especially in viewing the narrowness of the gap between theory and practice. Is this climate subject to major change in the foreseeable future? Far too little time has passed under the new Soviet leadership for us to be sure whether the quality of science in agriculture can be expected to improve fundamentally. Some possible trends are visible, but to understand them clearly we need first of all to distinguish between productivity and creativity.

While engineering is seen as closely allied with productivity, that is, employing established knowledge to enhance material or social output, science is viewed as quite a different type of pursuit, one that is closely allied with creativity. Productivity, especially in modern complex urban economies, is largely a result of engineering systems in which organization and controls are the main keys to efficiency. If this view is essentially correct, there is no important difference between the private bureaucracy needed to organize the operation of a General Motors in the United States and the administrative apparatus needed to manage an industrial enterprise in the USSR. In short, there seems to be no fundamental reason why communist urban production enterprises cannot be run as efficiently as any Western corporation. Again, modern production systems demand tight control mechanisms to coordinate not only the individual input of many employees, sometimes hundreds of thousands, with each other, but to coordinate these with the machines that produce so large a part of an industry's output. On the production side, control in a General Motors system is nearly total. Therefore, totalitarian economic systems should be wholly compatible with, indeed ideally suited for, industrial production systems.

Creativity and science, however, are not compatible with such controls. Why? Unlike the demands for industrial efficiency, which depends largely upon the precise repetition of established patterns, the scientist (or artist) who is searching for new knowledge cannot know in the beginning of his quest all the ingredients (materials, men or formulas) that will be necessary to bring a new order out of the chaos of the unknown. Plentiful evidence on this point was given in Whyte's study of *The Organization Man*, where the author recorded that the vast majority of basic discoveries in the United States have been achieved in the research climate found in university and independent laboratories, and not by scientists employed in corporation research where some of the controls essential for the production side of the firm inevitably spill over into the research laboratories. Therefore, most basic research in Western societies is divorced from production and its related responsibilities. In contrast, the organization of Soviet research in agriculture seems much more nearly to resemble that of the Western corporation research and development operations and their close ties to production achievements and profit.

In the realm of the natural sciences, the lessons of Lysenkoism have had an important impact. If rigidly enforced, the demand that new discoveries must be scientifically tested should discourage the rise of new frauds in agricultural science. However, even in this seemingly less controversial realm of science (as contrasted with the social sciences), several old shadows of doubt persist. First of all, Soviet scientists must still give priority to ideology. The President of the All-Union Academy of Agricultural Sciences stresses the following as 'necessary' to raising the 'theoretical level' of research: 'The most important method of overcoming shortcomings lies in a closer contact with life, practice, the profound creative use of Marxist–Leninist agrarian theory, the objective economic laws of socialism and a decisive improvement of the methods of economic research.'[17]

Secondly, in regard to the distinction made above between the demands of creativity and productivity, doubt is raised by the continuing stress in the literature upon the closeness of 'theoretical and applied' research. Indeed, a call by Premier Kosygin to establish 'direct economic accountability' between the laboratories and production enterprises[18] implies that precisely those blocks to discovery that are blamed for the paucity of basic scientific findings in Western corporation laboratories are about to be imposed. A field research station that goes too long without producing a valuable new plant hybrid, or a corporation lab that exists for years without showing a way of increasing profits, is in danger of having its financial support reduced, perhaps removed altogether.

Finally, the most gloomy of the lingering shadows on agricultural science is an indication that the leadership still tends to pass judgements in the technical realm. Perhaps Khrushchev's greatest mistake in agricultural affairs was his repeated insistence upon telling the farms in one area to grow corn, and those in another area to grow peas, or to argue that science supported a particular type of cultivation. In total, such actions merit the subsequent charges of 'subjectivity', and the revival of 'the cult of personality'. Perhaps, however, his acts were more a reflection of an inescapable weakness in the Soviet leadership system than an expression of his particular personality. Whatever the cause of Khrushchev's intervention in realms beyond his competence, however, the point is that even if agricultural scientists must be expected to err occasionally in their technical judgements, on such matters a wise leadership must accept the fact that the agricultural specialists will be more often right than the leaders. Moreover, if enthusiastic contribution from the scientists is to be encouraged, their judgement must be accepted in technical matters, unless overriding political or economic considerations clearly call for an alternate course of action. Indeed, in the new leadership's attempt to encourage science in agriculture, the adoption of just such an attitude towards decision-making has been stressed, at least in theory. Unfortunately, practice reveals something else.

In his May 1966 speech on the new land improvement programme, Party Secretary Brezhnev, claiming the support of one segment of Soviet scientific opinion, declared that 'we cannot agree with' those Soviet agricultural scientists who believe there is a 'lack of experience in cultivating cereals on irrigated land',[19] or in other words, that cereals are not the best crops to grow on it. Brezhnev, however, insists that they are: his list includes corn and rice, but he emphasizes wheat. Certainly, special irrigation techniques used in the United States have increased the yields of small grains significantly, but in most instances where the expensive investment in creating irrigation systems has been made, other crops such as corn, rice, alfalfa or vegetables can be cultivated more profitably than small grains. The decision to invest vast sums in the development of irrigation systems is, of course, a central political responsibility. But whatever the scientific truth in regard to specific Soviet needs, Brezhnev's insistence upon growing certain crops goes beyond the realm of his technical competence, and thus he has repeated a weakness of his predecessors.[20] The morale of agricultural scientists who disagree with the Brezhnev point of view has suffered, and, as happened so often when Khrushchev took sides in order to promote his campaigns, at least some technically incompetent local party leaders can now be expected to exploit Brezhnev's authority and to override any local specialists who might argue that given the needs and conditions of a particular area, valuable irrigated land would be more efficiently used for crops other than wheat.

As noted earlier, although a new landmark seems to have been set in the application of social science finding to agriculture, because such research is so much more closely allied to the controversial and touchy realms of ideology and politics than are the natural sciences, further advance here probably will be even more difficult.

The new leadership is surely right in deciding that future increases in food output must come from increased yields. However, where is the solid evidence, that social science should be able to provide, to support the ever-increasing stress upon very large specialized farms, given Soviet needs and conditions ? However often Soviet apologists cite examples of American farms, which may be large when contrasted with most other agricultural systems but for the most part are tiny alongside the huge Soviet *kolkhozy* and *sovkhozy*, it remains true that in the relatively land-rich and labour-poor economic environment of the United States there is little analogous with the Soviet setting. Questions of farm size and organization are the most crucial for the future of agriculture in communist societies, and it is disturbing that studies documenting the surprising increases in output as a result of the *zveno* experiments (see Chapter 6 below) now seem to have been discredited in a manner that would be unacceptable to Western social science standards.[21]

THE 'NEO-MALTHUSIAN CAMP'

Perhaps our increasing concern over the parallel problems of the population explosion and the lagging increases in world food output has unscientifically coloured our judgement, but with this confession made, the preponderance of Soviet writing on the food *v.* population problem seems to us to reflect what is still wrong with Soviet science in general, and science in agriculture in particular. Much of it still expresses great optimism as to the miracles that science must bring. But the peculiar Soviet scientific environment seems particularly vulnerable to the exaggerated claims of a new Lysenko or even of a Brezhnev taking sides among the scientists. Soviet writers are quite right to point to the great food reserves in the seas, and to remind us that if the average yield per hectare (2·45 acres) were raised but a few centners (1 centner equals 1·49 bushels of wheat) throughout the world, today's food supplies would be ample.[22] But they then charge Western scientists who stress the seriousness of the world food problem with belonging to an unsupportable 'neo-Malthusian camp'.[23] To see validity in the Malthusian view, however, one does not have to be blind to these output potentials. One may simply be acutely aware of the political, economic and ideological blocks to the practical development of new sources of food. A Soviet student of philosophy's dissent to the predominant 'neo-Malthusian' charge is heartening: 'The scientists who rightly claim that the earth can "feed" scores of billions of people often forget to

74

ask at what cost of labour, knowledge and capital, and at what cost of other aims Man has set for himself?'[24]

There are encouraging new stirrings in Soviet agricultural science. New levels of technological application in the nation's fields may well be in the making. Unfortunately, however, the Soviet scientist who wishes to concentrate on basic research seems to be stifled by an atmosphere quite unlike that enjoyed by his Western colleagues. Great reservoirs of potential creativity exist, but they are contained behind dams of political and ideological control that probably cannot be unleashed until fundamental changes are made in the system of rule.

CHAPTER 5

The Soviet Technical Potential: 1980

THE Union of Soviet Socialist Republics is the largest state in the world, and as a result there is much over-optimism and considerable misunderstanding about its food-producing potential. The over-optimism arises from assuming that material aid can achieve something without accompanying human change, and the misunderstanding, both within and without the USSR, from overestimating the seemingly unlimited land resources of that nation which encompasses the great bulk of the territory of the communist states.

TSARIST EXPORTS

As noted earlier, Tsarist Russia was a major exporter of grain. Can the fact that since the drought of 1963 the Soviet Union has had to import huge quantities of grain be attributed to communist mismanagement? Surely, had the communist leaders instituted different policies all this could have been avoided? However, Westerners who remember that Tsarist Russia exported grain seem to forget that over the same years, recurring famine caused repeated mass starvation among the peasants. Were Russian peasants so stupid that they did not have enough sense to save for the lean years, or was it that since the landlords controlled the great bulk of the food, grain was exported in surplus years when it should have been stored against years of crop failure? Even in good years the peasant diet hardly met proper nutritional standards. If Tsarist Russia had adopted programmes assuring all her people an adequate and balanced diet, one suspects there would have been little if any grain left for export to purchase Western machines for the factories and luxuries for the ruling few. On humanitarian grounds, therefore, Tsarist Russia probably should not have been the great grain exporter she was. Moreover, had her leaders adopted policies that would have assured the peasant masses adequate food, one of the motive forces of the 1917 revolution would never have come into being.

There is yet another false myth among the urban leaders of the world, that however poor peasants may be, however inadequate their hovels, at least they eat fairly well. Aren't they, after all, the producers of the food? Ironically enough, however, the great concentrations of hunger are in predominantly peasant nations (see Chapter 7). More than this, interviews with Indian economists support the opinion that even in that hungry nation, the diet of the rural poor is probably worse than that of the hungry masses of Bombay or Calcutta. Distribution of imported food is far more difficult among the less concentrated rural peoples. Where religion will permit animal protein in the form of meat and milk to be consumed, poor peasants can rarely afford to kill one of their precious larger animals for their own use, and in rural areas cold storage facilities are virtually nonexistent. Moreover, the world's land usage maps make it clear that the world's teeming peasant masses mostly live in agricultural areas where the primary crops are coffee, copra, or other agricultural products with little or no nutritive value. Under the best circumstances, most of the world's farmers do not have enough land for their own families' needs, let alone for large sales of produce to the cities. Where balanced intensive farming is practised, as it is in Poland, the peasants probably eat as well as, perhaps even better than, the urban workers, but such farming conditions are the exception rather than the rule. The Tsarist peasants were both hungry for land and hungry for food and they finally found the organizational strength to revolt. Many, perhaps most, of the nations of the world have peasant populations in a similar situation today, and the Soviet leaders are not all wrong in saying that the revolution of 1917 offers a model for present 'revolutions of national liberation'.

Turning directly to the Russian experience, and keeping in mind relative levels of technological advance, both Tsarist Russia in its day and Soviet Russia today have had more mouths to feed from a much less favourable agricultural base than has the United States. Indeed, the late Dr Lazar Volin estimated that perhaps only 25 per cent of all the land in the USSR is tillable, as compared to some 60 per cent of the land in the United States (which was roughly one third the size of the USSR before the addition of Alaska and Hawaii). Even in the tillable areas, the Soviet farms must often work against severe handicaps, and in a climate that is unenviable. The great Eurasian land mass, of which the USSR occupies the lion's share, has isolated most of its agricultural areas from the moderating and moisture-producing influences of the sea. Great tracts of land lie either north of the perma-frost line, or in arid semi-desert and desert regions in the south. One quarter of all of the Soviet Union has less than 16 inches of moisture a year, too little for cropping purposes. In short, as Dr Volin concluded, the Soviet farmer has a tougher time than his Western counterpart.[1]

Under communism the peasantry, given a hard row to hoe by nature, has nevertheless managed to increase yields. The great famine of the 1930s was man-made, caused largely by the disruption resulting from Stalin's forced collectivization drive, and again in 1949, another poor crop year, it was because of Stalin's decision not to import food that the people were left to starve. Khrushchev, however, faced with the same situation in 1963, decided to buy food abroad, refusing once again to follow Stalin's example.

KRUSHCHEV'S LEGACY

The Khrushchev era in agriculture is over. Life today in the USSR is better than it was in 1953, partly because until 1958, agricultural output was significantly advanced under his leadership. Unfortunately, however, the bulk of this achievement depended upon the speculative new lands and corn-growing ventures. Since both programmes were enormously over-extended, and after 1958 the depletion of the new land soils increased precipitously, further advance in food output, particularly the crucial grain crop, stagnated even though new agricultural investments, especially in fertilizer, were being pumped into the countryside.

Khrushchev, Russia's first peasant and first agricultural scientist rolled into one, devoted the vast majority of his time and effort to agriculture. His speeches on this subject numbered over two hundred. However, his major gamble that ploughing up some forty million hectares of arid land would solve the Soviet grain problem failed. After the fortuitous 1958 rainfall, the best in the virgin lands region for fifty years, grain yields in the area began to drop. Since advances in yields in the older areas had stagnated, the outlook for Soviet agriculture was alarming. Khrushchev announced his own intensification campaign during his final months in office, but the 1963 crop failure very likely precipitated his removal from power.

SOVIET IMPORTS

Barring some unforseen major technical breakthrough tha would allow enormous increases in grain yields per unit of land, Soviet food output can be expected to fall far short of the fantastically high goals Khrushchev originally set for 1980, the end of the current twenty-year planning period. True, 1966 was a bumper grain year, even better than 1958. However, such harvests are primarily a result of luck with the weather, and bad crop years such as 1963 will come again. Indeed, one of the first acts of the post-Khrushchev leadership was to abandon the unrealistic 1980 goals for agriculture, and make a deal with Canada for annual grain imports until the end of 1968. Without announcing new 1980 targets, Brezhnev and Kosygin established much more reasonable goals for 1970 than those implied in Khrushchev's plan. Perhaps the Western observer should ignore Khrushchev's goals too, but for one very important reason they are still of interest. Although Khrushchev never explained in public how his targets had been arrived at, recent population growth rates in the Soviet Union imply that these targets must be met if the projected 1980 population is at long last to enjoy Western nutritional standards. Although the people have not been going hungry in recent years, without enormous output increases and/or enormous new imports the protein content of the Soviet diet is destined to remain far below that of Western diets; recently it was about half the level of North American consumption of animal protein.[2] The tendency for Soviet ladies to run to dumpling shapes is a reflection of their need to substitute starch for protein.

Unfortunately, again assuming no major technical advance in production methods and constant rates of population growth, a case can be made, using yields recently achieved in North America as the basis of measurement, that output per capita may even decline. The possible implications of this bleak outlook, in terms of both Soviet domestic and international affairs and the need of the world for more food, are highly significant.* The new Soviet administration, as indicated, has pared down the 1970 goal of grain production to a more reasonable 167 million metric tons, but even if the new goal is achieved,

---

* These and later conclusions are summarized from documented research findings originally published elsewhere.[3] This research was conducted with several important assumptions and conditions which are explained in Appendix A along with further supporting data.

given the present growth-rate of the population, this amount of grain will not support the meat and milk production necessary to raise the protein content of the Russian people's diet to the hoped-for level. But can the Soviet Union accomplish the new 1970 goal ? Given the purely technical side, perhaps they can, if the following requirements are met:

1. That the marginal new lands areas equal or better the yields produced on comparable land in Saskatchewan, Canada (used for comparison by Carl Zoerb in his excellent new lands study).[4]

2. That corn-producing regions, with increased irrigation and fertilization, can match United States corn yields.

3. That established farming areas sown to small grains can achieve at least 90 per cent (allowing for less favourable growing conditions in the USSR) of the United States yields.*

Assuming that these qualifications could be met, we illustrate in Table 2 below our conclusion that technically the USSR could produce as much as 170 million metric tons of grain per year by 1970, which is quite in line with the stated goal. We further project that 214 million tons seems to be the maximum possible production per year by 1980, considerably short of Khrushchev's original figure of 300 million tons.

Such a technical projection, however, makes no allowance whatsoever for any difference in output efficiency between North American and Soviet farms. As documented in the chapter that follows, whereas the technical estimate based on American achievement would fall nearly one third short of the projected nutritional needs by 1980, even this level is unrealistic in light of output losses that must be expected from the continuation of the present collectivized system.

* See Appendix A for a more detailed explanation of these points.

Table 2

YIELDS OF ALL GRAINS: 1970 AND 1980 GOALS

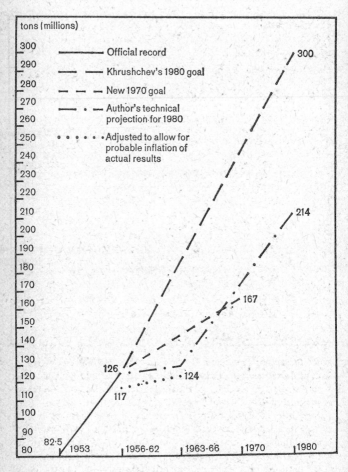

Table 3

YIELDS OF CORN AND SMALL GRAINS

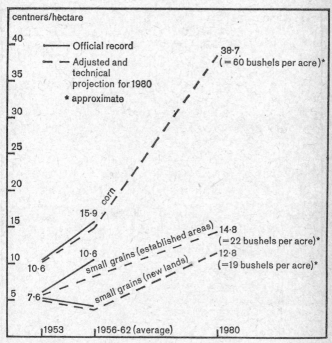

centners/hectare

— Official record

— — Adjusted and technical projection for 1980

* approximate

38·7 (= 60 bushels per acre)*

corn

15·9

10·6

small grains (established areas) 14·8 (= 22 bushels per acre)*

small grains (new lands) 12·8 (= 19 bushels per acre)*

7·6

1953   1956-62 (average)   1980

Since the author first made these projections, the Soviet statisticians have again repeated their disturbing practice of changing the base for reporting data. As a result, corn that does not ripen, reported in terms of grain equivalents between 1956–62, is no longer counted (surely an improvement) and regional data that allowed for a separate accounting of the new lands yields and yields in established areas has been changed (a disappointment). Therefore, the post-1962 record of what is presented here probably cannot be extended. However, the graph still reflects the base of the author's original projections as opposed to the 1956–62 record.

CHAPTER 6

The Price of Collectivization

THE hugeness and industrialization in agriculture to which ideological and political considerations have committed the communist states are costing them enormous losses in food output. These two criteria are incompatible with the needs and demands of the farming operation, which for maximum efficiency must be of such a size and structure that the management can be aware of all farm activity at all times and make the on-the-spot decisions required by constantly changing conditions. Obviously, then, to maximize their agricultural production, communist states should alter their farming system. Indeed, there has been some hope that the long delay in the promulgation of the New Model Charter for Agricultural Artels (promised in the autumn of 1964) implies that fundamental changes in the Soviet agricultural system are in the making, but blocks to such a change are great. Political demands on communist agriculture seem destined to block any major future success such as might be hoped for from the new agricultural intensification programme. True, as of the time of writing, the new leadership has avoided making decisions in Moscow that efficiency demands should be made on the farms, and Khrushchev's penchant for issuing directives to cultivate in a certain manner here and to sow a particular crop there has not been generally copied, but this is not enough.

INDUSTRY v. AGRICULTURE

An important change is occurring in Soviet industry. Profit is supplanting plan fulfilment as the prime measure of industrial success. Modern communist leaders are admitting that without proper investment coupled with adequate incentives arising from profit, efficient industrial management cannot be expected. Thus suffering the embarrassment of changing Marxian doctrine to fit profit motivation, Soviet industry has started down the road pointed out by Professor Liberman and his colleagues. Why not similar changes for agriculture ? As painful as adopting profit for Soviet industry has proved to be, the political and ideological cost of this innovation has been very small when compared to the possible cost of the alterations necessary to cure agriculture's ills, for the latter would mean giving up the ideological and political advantages of the present system discussed in earlier chapters.

On the ideological side, Marx had argued that however much industry may dehumanize the worker by chaining him to his machine, the industrial revolution must be accepted since only machines can produce enough material goods for the whole of society to enjoy. As implied earlier, however, Marx, later followed by Lenin, went too far. Theoretically, they argued, the methods by which urban industry achieves great output advances can be directly transferred to agriculture. A key doctrine behind the establishment of the Soviet collectives rested upon Lenin's staunch arguments that machine processes allow a fundamental breakthrough in agricultural output, and that peak efficiency in mechanized farming can be achieved only when industrial organizational and administrative patterns are adopted on the farms. To illustrate a major flaw in this Marxist–Leninist argument, let us examine the needs of agriculture in light of Marx's use of 'congealed working time' in his theory of value.

Marx held the view (partially correct) that the value of a product was equal to the number of labour hours necessary for its production. Once a production line is established, modern industry uses much less labour and requires much less judgement and worker skill (which Marx's theory tended to ignore) per unit of production than does agriculture. For example, a mechanized factory can turn out hundreds of thousands of nails for only a dollar's (or rouble's) worth of direct labour expenditure. Apart from the engineering, administrative and sales forces that are not directly engaged in production, and the minimal labour needed to maintain the machines, little training is required to operate them, and human hands do very little on the production line. In complete contrast to industry, agricultural production requires much more 'congealed worker time' and much more worker judgement and individual attention. If a farmer is not properly skilled or sufficiently interested to treat his plants and animals with considerable care, these highly perishable products can be seriously damaged or destroyed. A worker in an automated nail factory might set his machine wrong and produce a batch of nails that are too short. Yet, at worst, time is lost, for the metal can be melted and used again. An unskilled or careless tractor driver, however, who runs his cultivator over a row of corn, has destroyed a portion of the crop that can never be replaced. Stated simply, therefore, the industrially organized *sovkhozy* and *kolkhozy* discourage peasant attention to production needs, a state of affairs that is directly traceable to errors inherent in Marxist–Leninist theory when applied to agricultural practice.

POLITICS AND DECISION-MAKING ON THE FARM

Not only have Marxist–Leninist theories led to the imposition of impossible production patterns upon Soviet farm managers, but as noted earlier, the political system they fostered has meant that, unlike farms in most other societies, the *sovkhozy* and *kolkhozy* also encompass the primary unit of local government as well as the place of work and the home. In other societies there is a great overlapping of economic and political factors in agriculture, but on the Soviet farms, economic and political decision-making are totally integrated in the same farm administration that is responsible at the same time for the production achievement on thousands of hectares and for governing the affairs of some two thousand people who live on the average *kolkhozy*. The fact that Soviet farm managers need to devote much of their effort to political control in the name of a central will is surely a serious additional drain upon production efficiency.

Near the end of his bumptious career as the USSR's first peasant, Khrushchev made two highly revealing observations on the cost of the *kolkhoz-sovkhoz* political system. In the process of his campaign to encourage a several-fold increase in the production of much needed fertilizer, he noted 'our leaders treat fertilizer as if it were a burden', and complained that in his travels about the country he often saw huge piles of that precious commodity just lying out on the ground along the railroads.[1] Fertilizer that is properly cared for and applied is gold for the farm manager whose primary concern is production efficiency. Obviously, *kolkhoz* chairmen who leave scarce fertilizer lying out in the weather are not concentrating all their efforts on maximizing yields. Similarly, drawing upon the lessons of his visit to America, Khrushchev observed that *rayon* (district) technical officials offered the *kolkhozy* the same benefits received by the American farmer from his county agent.[2] Unfortunately, however, the Soviet official can, if he feels the need, impose his will on the farms, and the history of Soviet collectivization is full of examples of well-meaning outside authorities insisting on having their way, often in ignorance of on-the-farm conditions that render such demands nonsensical and sometimes harmful. On the other hand, perhaps the main key to the enormous success of the American county agent is that the independent farmer can take or reject the agent's advice, acceptance being determined by the farmer's judgement of his particular needs and the degree of confidence he has in the agent. These differences still exist, for the agricultural system initiated by Stalin and brought to its logical conclusion by Khrushchev remains essentially intact at the beginning of the 1970s.

The controlled conditions of a modern industrial plant can allow a manager to make crucial production decisions, even though he is a continent removed from the scene. In contrast, successfully responding to unpredictable changes in the season or in plants and animals is the essence of efficient agricultural production. Therefore, timely sowing, harvesting, and caring for animals often contradicts the best-laid plans because some crucial element of the work environment has changed. Yet Khrushchev attempted to impose Moscow-made decisions on farms in Kazakhstan and Latvia when, in fact, even the chairman of a huge *kolkhoz* in these areas could not have all the instant knowledge needed to run his own farm efficiently, without delegating much authority to men in the fields and the barns.

The changing demands of nature and the peculiar needs of growing things are universal; therefore, whether in the US or the USSR, if the cows have broken into the corn, management must give first priority to driving them out and repairing the fences. If a *kolkhoz* chairman has insisted that *all* changes in work orders must come from him, and he is ten kilometres away in his office, great losses can occur before the orders are given and men are found to collect the cattle and mend the fences. It is true that because most of the contingencies involved have been brought under control, modern poultry production has been successfully transformed into what is essentially a highly efficient, enclosed, industrial operation. However, with all the aids that the industrial revolution has brought to farming, most agricultural operations remain out of doors and cannot be effectively industrialized until man finds the means of imposing the close tolerances on nature (thus on most of the countryside) that he builds into his machines and factories.

Human caprice can have much more impact on the strictly

production side of agriculture than it has on the carefully planned operation of an assembly line. An automobile worker may take the day off to go fishing and his work be taken up by another employee, but a farmer's neglect of his fields for even a day, at crucial seasons, could make the difference between profit and loss in a whole year's work. As long as the assembly line operates, an auto worker can be virtually certain that tomorrow, and a year from now, he will be fitting doors to car bodies. On a farm, if it is harvest season, the day's plan may be to harvest grain, but if a heavy rain hits, not only will combines be unable to operate, but the farmer may have to turn to quite different tasks such as finding dry storage for recently delivered fertilizer. The choice of a particular task at a particular time must be made from a long list of possible priorities since, for example, the same rain might also be of great value in refilling a depleted stock pond, if an hour or two can be spared to repair a damaged levee.

Viewed from the outside, farms seem to reflect the placid rural scenes often painted by landscape artists, and most of the time most of the work is tedious routine. Yet if no one is there to respond instantly when the situation does change, the results can be disastrous, and a huge, bureaucratically organized farm that blocks the initiative of the workers who are directly responsible for the plants and animals can never make the most of the changing environment of agricultural production.

The success of a Scottish crofter or an independent Polish peasant farmer can be crucially influenced by governmental action. Political decisions affecting prices could cause such a farmer to sell his sheep and turn to poultry raising. However, within the boundary of their farms, relative success or failure is determined primarily by the farmers' skill in balancing the potential of their land against changing natural conditions. For such farmers there exist challenges, opportunities and frustrations in their work that are largely unknown to the industrial worker or to either the hired hand on an American corporate farm or a peasant in a *kolkhoz* brigade. According to economic theory, there are three determinants of efficiency: land, labour and capital. However, timeliness in making decisions is also crucial to agricultural success. The Soviet Union has the land (although poorer than that in most Western countries) and the labour. And, since 1964, the resolution to increase agricultural investment significantly implies that adequate levels of capital may be forthcoming. But in his decision-making the average *kolkhoz* chairman or *sovkhoz* director remains saddled with a managerial monstrosity. He has to make decisions that should be made by the peasants dealing directly with the plants and the animals, so that on large farms employing hundreds of workers, not only is the individual peasant denied the satisfaction of personal initiative in his work, but crucial decisions that may demand instant answers must await word from higher authority. In making this study we asked numerous state and collective farm managers in Poland, Yugoslavia and Mexico about peasant initiative in day-to-day decision-making. Invariably the answer echoed one manager's response: 'No, a herdsman can't change the amount of feed or the time of feeding for the cattle under his charge . . . he must do what he's told.'

Apart from lacking the satisfaction of exercising initiative in his work, the collective farmer recognizes that most of his income (and any bonuses for state farm workers, where wages have been guaranteed) is not directly dependent upon the quality of his own work. The Soviet *kolkhoz* peasant's work has been recorded in terms of 'labour-days' (*trudodny*), which in practice are really piece-work units rather than measures of time. Each Soviet farm has to classify thousands of such units into specific categories of relative value. Thus every farm has to devote enormous expense to checkers, who each day must verify the work accomplished by each of the peasants, and bookkeepers to keep track of the accounts. The actual end value of a peasant's *trudodny*, however, is not predictable at the time the work is performed because the roubles paid per unit of work ultimately depend upon the successes and failures of the farm for the year. All over the world farmers must suffer the caprices of the weather, but in communist states they are additionally dependent upon the skill of the administration and the value of the effort of hundreds of their fellow workers. Moreover, under such circumstances the peasant's daily tasks are bureaucratically assigned, and, for example, although the best interests of the farm might be served by his leaving a tractor to make emergency repairs in a leaking irrigation ditch, every hour spent in such activity could mean that many hours less applied to his labour-day earnings.

Marx correctly saw that the price of industrial efficiency was the dehumanization of the worker, figuratively chained to his machine. How ironic it is that farms created in the name of his ideas virtually chain millions of peasants to their tedious tasks, and instead of productive gains, there is actually a loss in efficiency.

OPTIMUM SIZE AND OUTPUT

Agricultural production demands differ from those in industry in yet another way. Not only is timeliness in decision-making vital, but also in many important instances only the agricultural production worker himself can have the grasp of the situation that is necessary if farm production is to succeed. This is why the size of a farm, as related to the particular production needs and the talents of the manager, can be so important.

Although reared with Nebraska prejudices, the authors must confess that awe at the achievement of industrial miracles, the repeated claims for the achievements of corporate farms in the United States, and the glowing accounts of the successes of the Israeli *kibbutzim* have at one time made them doubt the above assertions, and think that perhaps, led by communist example, large industrial farms would shortly supplant the independent, manager-operated farms. It seemed as though the question could be resolved if the production efficiency of various types and sizes of farms under similar conditions could be compared.

In the search for evidence, one of our most important early discoveries was an Iowa State University study done in the late 1950s by Professor Earl O. Heady and his colleagues. In it similar farms in north central Iowa using grain–meadow rotations were compared, the only difference being size. The larger farms were almost as big as the huge, and assertedly superior, industrial farms. The study shows that profits did rise sharply on farms up to 440 acres, and continued to increase slightly on those between 440 and 880 acres. For farms over 880 acres in size, however, not only did profits per acre fall, but yields of grain fell off as well, due to a lack of 'timeliness in operations'.[3] This same work reported that the contribution of the largest farms in the nation (the industrial farms) to the total food output had been declining in the most recent period studies. Moreover, in his independent study, Professor Theodore W. Schultz discovered that over the extended period of 1929–60 farm rent and mortgage payments also indicate a growth in the relative importance of the independent farmer.[4]

Still, lessons from Iowa and the United States were perhaps not universally applicable, and needed testing in other countries where soil, climate, political and economic conditions were different. Supported in 1966 by a National Science Foundation grant the authors carried out a small pilot study of a number of large collective *ejido* in rural Mexico. In 1967, although the Soviet authorities refused to issue a visa ('Vietnam' was the excuse given), a Fulbright grant to conduct the study in Yugoslavia and Poland was accepted by these nations, and we surveyed numerous farms with the aid of a standardized questionnaire. Most important of all, however, the excellent staff of the Warsaw-based Polish Institute for Agricul-

Economics presented us with a complete set of the statistical data for the two previous years, that the Institute compiles on a hundred representative PGR (state farms) and uses in its own analyses.[5]

Professor Schultz is quite right in asserting that there is nothing magic about farm size as such. However, if it is true that decision-making is vital in agricultural production, the optimum size for a given type of farm will be related to the limits within which managers can remain fully informed about changing environmental conditions. Although communist states have repeatedly experimented with communal management and democratic decision-making, they have universally settled upon the practice of one-man management in the name of production efficiency. Peasant-worker boards may participate in long-range planning sessions as they do in Yugoslavia and Poland, but, as noted earlier, the day-to-day operations on Eastern European and Soviet collective and state farms are under the direction of a single farm chairman or director who is assisted by a staff of specialists in charge of various major sections of the farm. Even though a farm director may be able to extend his efficiency by delegating some of the decision-making to his key assistants, overall efficiency depends upon his ability to direct and coordinate the entire operation. The major hypothesis of the study was that an optimum size for collectivized farms, although probably different from that of the US manager-operated farms, must exist, measurable in terms of profit, yields per hectare of crops, and output per hectare of animal produce.

Perhaps the most interesting findings from the data on the hundred Polish state farms (which is presented in more detail in Appendix B) are that when divided into groups of ten according to size, on all counts measured (with the exception of numbers of workers per hundred hectares) the smallest farms are significantly more efficient than the largest farms, and the smallest farms are even smaller than the optimum size revealed in the Iowa study. As discussed in Appendix B, the smallest of the Polish farms do enjoy an advantage in soil quality, and they also had more mineral fertilizer during the two-year period studied (which may have been a result of government distribution policy beyond the farms' control or, perhaps, a reflection of greater attention by the managers to this vital matter). Yet, when the smallest farms were compared with a control group of medium-sized farms, whose soil was as good as that of the smaller farms but had slightly more fertilizer, profits, yields per hectare of crops, and yields of animal produce all remained significantly higher on the smallest farms. Compared with the control group, averaging 502 hectares, the yield per hectare of grains on the smallest farms, averaging some 225 hectares, was 8 per cent more, yield of sugar beets was the same, but potatoes were 4 per cent higher, and milk produced per cow was 3 per cent greater, while the total live-weight of animals per hectare was 12 per cent more and the profit per hectare was 33 per cent greater.* More than this, during the visit to Warsaw, the authors obtained a published copy of a somewhat similar study done in 1961 by Dr J. Kosicki of a group of farms in the Poznan area.[6] The material presented in his monograph does not seem as conclusive as our analysis of the Institute statistics. Indeed, in his study, milk per cow increased with the size of the farm, although the number of animals per hundred hectares fell. Furthermore, rather than profit as such he gives figures of costs v. income which imply that the increase in income on the smaller farms was paralleled by cost increases. However, his analysis of field crop yields reveals a basic agreement with the picture presented in the statistics cited above. A comparison of the yield statistics contained in the two studies is presented in Table 4 below.

* Thereby more than justifying a labour force on the smaller farms that is 6 per cent greater than the number of workers per hundred hectares in the control group.

Table 4

YIELDS PER HECTARE ON SMALL
FARMS *v.* LARGE FARMS

(small farms = 100)

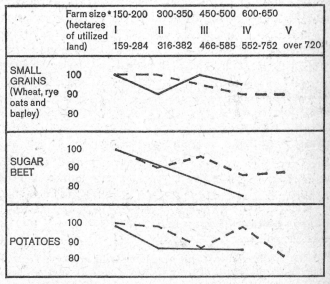

Farm size*	150-200	300-350	450-500	600-650	
(hectares of utilized land)	I	II	III	IV	V
	159-284	316-382	466-585	552-752	over 720

——— Kosički study   — — — Authors' study

* Groups I to IV are those studied by Dr Kosicki. Although the ten groups in the authors' study contain none that are exactly identical with the Kosicki groups, groups that were virtually the same as his four groups are presented here for purposes of comparison. As shown in the tables in Appendix B, the authors' groups 1 and 2 are used here for I and II, while groups III, IV and V here, are averages of groups 5 and 6, 7 and 8, and 9 and 10 in the Appendix tables. Although the Kosicki study contained farms only up to 650 hectares in size, the authors' study continues to farms of 1,285 hectares, the 'over 720' group here.

Since the analysis attempts to eliminate all other influences over efficiency, timeliness of decision-making must be the reason why the farms in the smallest group are the most efficient producers. Moreover, this same factor must also account for the fact that the most productive Polish farms are smaller than the optimum size farms in the Iowa study. Although they are smaller in area, they are much more intensively cultivated than the Iowa farms, combining major field and livestock operations and, often, vegetable produce, in contrast to the more specialized Iowa farms. Similarly, whereas the farmer on an Iowa farm usually had, beyond his own field work, no more than the work of two or three additional hands (mostly his own family's) to direct, the average director of the most efficient Polish farms employs some forty workers.

From this substantial evidence, then, we can begin to assess the cost to the communist states of full collectivization. Since the average Soviet *kolkhoz* and *sovkhoz* is several times larger than the largest and most inefficient Polish farms studied, the implication is that the price the Soviets pay for their system is upwards of a fifteen per cent loss in total output. Indeed, applying the over ten per cent loss of the larger farms in grain yields to the previously cited technically possible output of some 165–170 million metric tons of grain by 1970, unless the Soviets drastically overhaul their collectivized system they will be most fortunate to achieve an average annual output of over 155 million tons of grain in the near future. If the Soviet Union and other communist states with fully collectivized agricultural systems were producing food surpluses, the loss in yields would not be so crucial, or, if the collectivized systems proved to be saving in labour and management costs, perhaps they would be compensated for. Yet, according to the Soviet Union's own statistics, although agricultural labour output has been increasing somewhat, still in 1964 productivity of agricultural labour was only one fourth of that in the United

States.[7] Soviet statistics reveal further that administrative costs on their farms come to some fifteen per cent of total costs, costs that are largely non-existent on American farms since the manager–operator serves as his own administrator.[8]

Some of the published evidence in the long-smouldering Soviet controversy over the *zveno* becomes particularly important in light of the findings in the Polish state farm study. As described by one Soviet author, the independent *zveno* is a relatively autonomous unit that 'enters a *kolkhoz* or *sovkhoz* as a primary production unit', where it serves 'as an active owner'. In short, successes claimed for the small *zveno* depend upon breaking up the huge *kolkhozy* and *sovkhozy* into small units of several hundreds of hectares managed and worked by some half dozen individuals who often are from the same family. The following table gives results claimed for such an experimental division of the Ili state farm.[9]

	1962 (brigade system)	1963 (*zveno* system)
Total output of spring grain (tons)	3,150	9,204
Average annual number of workers	202	29
Grain output (centners) per worker	156	3,173
Wages (thousand roubles)	181	59

As noted earlier, such experiments have been roundly condemned as misleading by Soviet officials, just when they most need improved social science studies in agriculture. Perhaps the official comparative study undertaken by the Ukrainian Agricultural Academy rigidly adhered to the scientific method in finding that when 42 *zveno* were compared with brigades in the Ukraine, significantly higher yields were achieved by the brigades: 4 centners more of grain, 2·7 more of silage, and 27 centners more corn per hectare.[10]

Certainly there is a point in the Soviet critics' argument that the *zveno* are 'a throwback to private-property instincts ... [that] represent a fallacious non-socialist path'.[11] Nevertheless, as opposed to the conclusions from the Ukrainian study, the implications of American studies on optimum size are supported by the authors' study, the data in Dr Kosicki's earlier Polish study, and some of the Soviet's own *zveno* studies. Surely the balance of the social science evidence indicates that much of the lagging production of collectivized agriculture must be credited to the system itself.

However, this is not all the evidence. Before turning to an additional important piece of data, however, one point needs to be underlined. The authors are not partisans of small farms. The tiny parcels of land that comprise most of the farms in the world are a great human tragedy. Just as the evidence presented here indicates an enormous waste because even the best of farm managers cannot adequately cope with farms that are too huge and boast inflated farm bureaucracies, so similar evidence exists indicating waste arising from an under-use of human potential on farms that are too small. But, taken together, the evidence suggests that if societies must err, error on the too-small side is less costly to production results than error on the too-large side.

Understandably, statistical evidence that will allow meaningful comparisons of performance between collectivized farms and small independent peasant operations is very scarce in the USSR and Eastern Europe. Here again, however, the long and laudable social science tradition in Poland provides an important exception. In Poland, official statistics on performance in the private agricultural sector is published alongside that of the socialized sector, i.e., the state and collective ('cooperative')* farms.

In recent years great dissatisfaction with the bulk of the Polish collectives that existed prior to 1955 has resulted in a large number being eliminated, reducing the total from 9,790 in that year to only 1,268 in 1965. Only the very best of the collectives have survived, and the state farms now comprise the

* These are to be distinguished from the cooperatives ('circles') that serve the Polish private farmers.

great bulk of the land in the socialized agricultural sector, which claims about 15 per cent of the total. A comparison of the performance of the independent peasant farms with that of the socialized sector in 1965 (which is representative of performance in recent years) reveals that although the tiny parcels of land that comprise the private farms average only some 3 to 5 hectares, on balance they clearly out-perform the state farms and the cooperative farms, which average some 400 and 200 hectares respectively. Yet the socialized sector is much more favoured; by comparison it is highly mechanized and often subsidized. For example, artificial fertilizer has been in short supply, and official statistics reveal that the state farms have been receiving nearly twice as much per hectare of this precious material aid as have the private and cooperative farms (which are lumped together for statistical purposes, though the collectives undoubtedly have received the lion's share). The following table shows that in spite of much greater handicaps, the private farms out-produce the state farms in all major areas but grain yields. Similarly, they out-produce the collectives in all major areas excepting grain yields and potatoes (and in the latter, nearly equal the cooperatives in spite of their greater quantities of artificial fertilizer).[12] In fact, when potato yields are averaged for the years 1960–65, the private farms come out slightly better than the collectives.

What little evidence there is on the comparative productivity of private and collectivized agriculture in the other Eastern European countries and the USSR suggests that if fair comparisons were made (allowing for subsidies and greater availability of scarce material aids for the socialized sectors), what is true in Poland would be found true elsewhere.

Table 5

1965 PERFORMANCE OF PRIVATE *v.*
SOCIALIZED SECTOR
(Poland)

Farms	Fertilizer per hectare (kgs)*	Yields per hectare (centners)			Livestock per 100 hectares			
		Small grains	Potatoes	Sugar beets	Cattle	Pigs	Sheep	Horses
State	127·1	19·5	154	214	49·2	39·9	14·1	4
Collective	[more than]† 63·9	22	161	228	45·5	58·7	15·2	4·6
Private	[less than]† 63·9	19	158	266	52·5	75·4	16·2	15·1

* 1964–5   † Private and collective lumped together.

Part Three

INTERNATIONAL DIMENSIONS

CHAPTER 7

'A World Calamity'*

THE 1917 Bolshevik revolution in Russia was only the opening engagement in the mounting world-wide agrarian revolution that characterizes the twentieth century. When completed, the revolution may initiate greater changes than did the urban-centred industrial revolution of the nineteenth century. If the Third World War comes, it will probably be precipitated by agrarian revolt in the underdeveloped nations. However, if the Armageddon that threatens can be avoided, that bulk of mankind that lives in rural areas will have a chance of achieving greatly improved standards of living.

AFRICA, ASIA AND LATIN AMERICA

A press account of a USAID (Agency for International Development) study, published in 1965, indicates that some 'seventy per cent of children in less developed countries were undernourished or malnourished.... [And] about fifty per cent of all children up to six years old were labelled ... "seriously malnourished"'.[1] This human tragedy is deepening, for in recent years the growth-rate of population in the developing nations has threatened to outstrip the growth of food supplies. Moreover, the people in these nations comprise some seventy per cent of the total world population.[2] On humanitarian and political grounds the crisis in food production as related to the population explosion is, and will continue to be for the foreseeable future, mankind's greatest problem.

* Part of the material in the first few pages of this chapter first appeared in *The Triangle of Power Conflict and Accommodation: The United States, The Soviet Union and Communist China*, Jan S. Prybla (ed.), Pennsylvania State University, 1967, pp. 3–13.

For the world as a whole (excluding Mainland China because of a lack of available statistics), the United Nations Food and Agricultural Organization (FAO) reports that indices for food products in Latin America, the Far East, the Near East and Africa show very little increase since 1958-9. Moreover, taking the average production of 1952-3 to 1956-7 as 100, preliminary estimates were that food production in these nations fell from a 106 peak in 1964-5 to 102 in 1965-6; these numbers can be contrasted with the figure of 102 for the average of the pre-Second World War years.[3] Therefore, although agricultural production has continued to rise in these regions of the world, not only has rapid population growth cancelled out gains, but since it is increasing by an average of about 2·5 per cent per year, they would have needed an unprecedented increase of almost 7 per cent in their total food production in 1966-7 just to regain even the meagre per capita level achieved by 1964-5.[4] Estimates of future population expansion imply a rate of growth between now and 1980 that is roughly double that of the industrialized nations.[5] A United Nations study of the population outburst in Asia and the Far East notes that, 'The sheer bulk of the population in the ... region ... which (already) holds just over half of humanity in less than one eighth of the earth's land area confronts it with problems of unparalleled proportions.'[6] Latin America, which many might assume to be least hurt by the population explosion, is actually one of the worst off regions of the world. Dr Alberto Lleras Camargo, former president of Colombia, testified before a United States Senate subcommittee that, 'Latin America is breeding misery, revolutionary pressures, famine and many other potentially disastrous problems in proportions that exceed our imagination even in the age of thermonuclear war.'[7] Similarly, the Swedish economist Professor Gunnar Myrdal has argued that 'the world is moving swiftly toward something more than crisis – a world calamity'.[8] Even among the three major world powers, only the United States is in a secure position as regards the production of food. China, with a population of some 700,000,000, has one of the world's most serious agricultural problems. As documented in the foregoing pages, the Soviet Union cannot be expected to solve its major agricultural production problems in the foreseeable future.

While the failure to produce adequate quantities of food is by far the most serious aspect of the world's human problem, in a sense, hunger is only the major symptom of a much broader crisis. The average North American and Western European is an urban resident who has not only an adequate diet, but decent housing, labour-saving appliances, and good transportation (often by his own car), and he is literate. In contrast, the average citizen of that seventy per cent of mankind that lives in the developing nations is a peasant with an inadequate diet, earth for the floor in his hut, and at best burros or oxen to help till his fields and provide some transportation, and he is illiterate. More than this, the average peasant's fields are probably not his own, and even with his best efforts they are probably too tiny to support him and his family decently. Thus, under existing political and economic conditions, the majority of mankind can hardly even hope for a better future for themselves or their children. Even Mexico, the most advanced of the Latin American nations, and justly proud of the land reform of the 1930s, continues to have a most serious agricultural problem. The authors' 1966 summer survey in several parts of rural Mexico discovered that poverty in rural areas is still widespread, and the failure of continuing agricultural advances to keep up with rising peasant expectations could become explosive. Dedicated governmental officials trained in agriculture and working in the farming regions are seriously concerned over the need for faster advance. Indeed, one key agricultural official emphatically agreed that 'the

Mexican government must continue to run like hell, just to keep ahead of serious rural unrest that could well precipitate another revolution'.

Mass hunger is not new. The ancestors of today's inhabitants of Asia, Latin America, and Africa have long known recurring hunger and famine. However, it has largely disappeared from Europe and North America in the present century (Stalin's man-made famine of the early 1930s being an exception). It is the absolute difference between the persistent hunger of large numbers of peoples in the developing world and the nutritional well-being of peoples of the industrialized nations that is a relatively recent phenomenon, and constitutes the danger to world peace.

Modern technology has not only produced the enormous gap between the living standards of the have and have-not nations, but it has also evolved communications systems that tie all mankind together, systems which have stimulated the growth of the 'revolution in rising expectations' at an epidemic rate. For example, the technical capability of transporting massive quantities of food to starving nations must be credited with making the have-not peoples aware that their plight is not to be tolerated. Even though they may remain predominantly illiterate, the hungry of the world can no longer accept their suffering as natural or inevitable, when at the least they have been exposed to local leaders who have seen or heard of Western standards.

INTERNATIONAL RELATIONS

Three of the most important axioms of political science will support a contention that the hungry peasant majorities in the developing nations have become the most important political force in the world:

1. Basic economic needs are the primary determinants of political policies.

2. If the basic wants and needs of a society's masses are continually ignored, a revolutionary situation is produced.

3. International politics are primarily an extension of domestic interests on the world scene.

Traditionally the urban half of the world (48 per cent in 1960)[9] has seemed to be the dynamic centre of human life and direction, for the cities possess the great share of mankind's wealth. But the food of the world is controlled by the farmers, and as Lenin learned in 1921, peasant majorities are capable of dictating policy.

To have asserted at the beginning of the present century that the long-term needs and interests of the world's peasants would become the most important factor determining international affairs would have seemed absurd; this, however, was before modern communications and transport technology had reduced the world's distances to hours, and economic exchanges had made the world a highly interdependent unit. What we are saying, then, is that the mass of the world's rural poor comprise a gigantic and increasingly restless interest group whose needs must be met if their tragedy is not to precipitate the Third World War. If this is correct, a major new trend in world affairs has taken place in the twentieth century.

The size and scope of the First and Second World Wars and the importance of the major urban centres, particularly in Europe and North America, tend to lead the student of current history to conclude that the industrially advanced states have continued to dominate human affairs from 1900 to the present. Certainly, the urban industrial areas of the world do seem to have guided major events in the early decades of the century. Moreover, the major industrial powers, and especially the Soviet and American super-powers, obviously remain enormously influential, both in the world of diplomacy and in the realm of economic activity. Yet traditional diplomacy and industrial economic activity are much less important to that bulk of mankind that lives in Africa, Asia and Latin America than they are to the Western European and the North American.

A second look at important changes in world affairs since the Bolshevik revolution of 1917 make this major shift that has occurred even more obvious. Previously we have pointed out that the Soviet revolution had an enormous influence upon world affairs, and that it was successful because of a strange alliance between industrially oriented Marxists and desperate peasant masses who would no longer abide by old relationships. Indeed, similar strange alliances have been the key to successful communist revolutions wherever they have occurred. Communism, then, from Russia in 1917 to China in 1949 and to the renewed Vietnam war in the 1960s, has had its major impact on public opinion where rural unrest has been at a breaking point. Even a review of events in Cuba will reveal a revolutionary situation wherein rural dissatisfaction played a key part, first in Castro's seizure of power and later in his success in continuing his hold over that island's government. These communist revolutions, important as they have been in the twentieth century, have been but the most impressive manifestation of generally widespread peasant discontent.

Leaders, both in the East and the West, have soberly suggested that food-short, overpopulated India with her predominantly peasant population is destined to remain a tinderbox. In many, perhaps most, developing nations, local leaders and outside observers alike have repeatedly argued that agrarian reform is an essential first change if disaster is to be avoided. As documented earlier, peasant discontent is the crucial factor in most Latin American countries. In contrast, Mexico's relatively higher standard of living and greater stability can be traced directly to a revolution that resulted in major agrarian reform. In Asia, similar observations can be made about the Philippines and, ironically, Formosa – having learned the power of peasant unrest on the mainland, Chiang

Kai-shek presided over important agrarian reform on that island. Yet these somewhat more advanced countries are still plagued by serious agrarian problems.

For the communist nations, agricultural problems have remained of primary concern. Lenin's New Economic Policy of 1921 granted concessions to the peasants' interests, largely to forestall the possibility of another revolt and the end to the Soviet experiment. Stalin's forced collectivization of the 1930s left Khrushchev and his successors with one of the world's most inefficient agricultural systems. In China the primary cause of the enormous failure of the 1957-8 'great leap forward' was the peasants' inability to adapt to the agricultural communes. Although the Sino–Soviet split is a highly complex affair involving conflicting nationalisms, ideological disputes, power conflicts and leadership jealousies, a combination of Soviet unwillingness and inability to give massive agricultural aid to hungry China must have been a major factor in deepening the rift between the two powers.

On the African continent, although a knowledge of biblical history and an awareness of the depth that nationalistic antagonisms can reach is necessary to understand the continuing Arab-Israeli wars, the plight of the predominantly rural Arab peoples, poor in tillable land and water, is surely a fundamental irritant in that long and dangerous struggle. Farther south, the earlier Congo crisis and the Biafran tragedy at the end of the 1960s focussed world attention and concern upon the plight of agrarian people.

However incomplete the above review of the major areas of world concern, particularly since the Second World War, it supports the assertion that the focus has shifted from the world's urban industrial centres to largely peasant, agricultural and developing nations. The earlier Berlin crisis and the Soviet–Czech crisis of August 1968 were exceptions to this pattern. True, the major powers' economic and military might has increased enormously, but the confrontations in Korea and

Vietnam and the crises over the Congo, Cuba and the Dominican Republic have revealed a great reluctance to use military power to the full. Clearly it can no longer guarantee a major power complete dominance over a weaker one.

The capitals of the major world powers have in fact lost most of the initiative in international affairs. Moscow and Washington DC can astound mankind with their men and ships in outer space, and both are capable of unleashing Armageddon, but in the changed affairs of the earth-bound it appears that the have-not rural majority of mankind constitutes a vital new focal point of initiative. Increasingly, the powers that once led now only respond, out of fear that if the demands of the world's rural people are not heard, a new Congo or Vietnam could result in a war that could destroy all that man has achieved. Perhaps a new 'green uprising' will dominate the rest of the twentieth century, as the industrial revolution dominated the latter half of the nineteenth century.

'WARS OF NATIONAL LIBERATION'*

Except in the fortunate regions of the world where past history has been kind to the rural populations, agriculture has long needed the revolution that now seems to be upon it. As stressed previously, most developing nations can be characterized as land-poor and labour-rich. Therefore, most of all they need increased yields from the soil that can come only if the agricultural system is properly organized and the peasantry have the knowledge and skills to exploit all possible aids to production. Critical shortcomings in education, systems of land tenure, and related factors of rural sociology comprise the most serious impediment to food output increases. Profound social and administrative changes must come first, or at least simultaneously, if the now predominantly illiterate peasants in

*Much of the material in this section was first prepared as a joint paper with a colleague, Professor Jaroslaw Piekalkiewicz.

the developing nations are to make efficient use of new scientific and technical aids. Moreover, if such changes are not made peacefully, largely indigenous communist revolutions can be expected eventually to encompass most of the developing nations, as they have already gained power in some. The British writer David Mitrany was the first to describe vividly this causal relationship when he wrote in 1951:

> The startling fact is that Communism has only come to power [by revolution] where by all Marxist tenets it might have been least expected that it could. In every instance, from 1917 in Russia to 1949 in China, Communism has ridden to victory on the back of disaffected peasantries; in no instance has it come near to victory in industrialized 'proletarian' countries. So far it has always been a 'proletarian' revolution without a proletariat; a matter of Communist management of peasant discontent.[10]

The Communists have continued to exploit agrarian revolutionary situations successfully since 1949. Castro's Cuba fits the general pattern. Whatever the changed character of the war in Vietnam, the early widespread support of the revolt in rural South Vietnam came from 'disaffected peasantries' who may not have known the difference between Karl Marx and Charles de Gaulle, but were receptive to a Marxist–Leninist inspired leadership that convincingly promised agrarian revolution. To date, leadership in the major Western democracies has failed to come up with an answer to this communist challenge. Moreover, within the developing nations themselves, local leadership also has failed, with such rare exceptions as Mexico, the Philippines and Formosa. Therefore, as of now, although communist leaders often fail too, their successes have been notable, and they have retained a virtual monopoly among those bidding for leadership in the developing nations because their promises of genuine agrarian reform carry conviction. Perhaps the peasants will eventually be forced on to collective farms as they were in the USSR, but a consistent factor of all communist revolutions has been a promise to redistribute the land, backed initially by concrete help in the peasants' long struggle against the landlords.

Lenin must be credited with being a major prophet of the future. The lessons of the 1905 rehearsal of the Bolshevik revolution in Russia brought home to him the realization that success must ultimately depend upon the positive role of the peasantry. Thus, as he wrote in his *To The Rural Poor*:

> What is the *class struggle*? It is the struggle of one part of the people against the other, the struggle waged by all the disfranchised, the oppressed, the toilers, against the privileged, the oppressors, the parasites; the struggle of the wage labourers, or proletarians, against the property owners, or bourgeoisie. In the rural districts of Russia, too, this great struggle has always gone on and is now going on although not everyone is aware of it, and although not everyone realizes its significance.[11]

The communists learned how to employ local government and the peasant masses in revolutionary conditions in their own hard classroom of history, the Russian Civil War, although at the same time they have shown and continue to show an extremely intelligent adaptability to local conditions in each separate case. The so-called Bolshevik revolution of 1917 was in fact only a *coup d'état* by a tiny handful of dedicated communists who captured the major cities in the midst of a sea of relatively undirected peasants that were revolting against their landlords in the countryside. The revolution was not secured over the whole of Russia until after the civil war that was to rage for the next three years. Communism's survival, therefore, depended upon devising a means of capturing the allegiance of the peasantry. By the summer of 1918 White Russian forces of various shades, plus foreign interventionists from several nations, had gathered on the periphery of the Bolshevik centre intending (to use Churchill's famous phrase) to 'strangle Bolshevism in its cradle'. A lack of will upon the part of the interventionists and a lack of coordination among the White forces certainly contributed to their failure, but perhaps in the final analysis, Lenin's political skill directed at the rural population was decisive.

'Committees of the Poor'

The Bolsheviks were faced with two problems: how to win the political support of the peasantry in their war against the Whites and the foreign interventionists; and how to obtain from the same peasants enough food to feed the city worker and particularly the Red Army. On the surface these two goals were dramatically contradictory as the peasants were not at all willing to sell their products for worthlessly inflated roubles, Red or White. But the Bolsheviks won on all fronts by skilful propaganda and organization of the communist local government in their own territory as well as in the lands temporarily occupied by the Whites, government which was headed by a few party zealots and supported by the committees of the village poor.

The propaganda-kindled peasant feared that a White victory would mean a return of the land to the former landlords who were supported in their endeavour by the 'foreign devils' determined to crush 'Mother Russia'. Through the fluctuating conditions of the civil war local government was organized on the basis of village 'soviets', which provided the communists with formal authority in the countryside, even if their actual power was nothing more than the psychological impact on the peasants' minds. This impact was however considerable, and by exploiting the fears and hatred of the peasants, the communists set the village poor, grouped into 'thirty thousand committees of the poor' (according to an official Soviet history text),[12] against the rural rich, the so-called *kulak* segment of the peasantry. The committees of the poor were then encouraged to enforce food requisitions, and were invaluable, as Lenin recorded, in helping to collect 'every particle of surplus grain for the state reserves, [so that] the whole country [was] swept clean of concealed or ungarnished grain surpluses'.[13]

A less astute leadership could easily have failed to glean hidden surpluses from a peasantry long practiced in concealing their small hoards from Tsarist officialdom. This problem was shrewdly solved, however, by harnessing the natural jealousy of the very poor and the shiftless to the cause; the hungry peasant knew only too well the hiding places and the tax-dodging ruses of his more fortunate neighbour and thus was an ideal tax gatherer.

The British historian E. H. Carr has argued, in *The Bolshevik Revolution*, that perhaps even more important than getting the food from the peasants, Lenin's committees of the poor were designed as a means 'to split the peasantry', thereby diminishing the possibility of their taking concerted political action.[14] Carr undoubtedly has a point, but beyond this, the committees constituted what government there was in the countryside, and were under the guidance of a disciplined party cadre. As noted in an earlier chapter, the importance of this technique and the communists' flexibility in adapting it to varying needs was emphatically demonstrated by Stalin in the forced collectivization of the late 1920s and early 1930s.

Stalin himself admitted that the forced collectivization of the countryside was 'a revolution from above' imposed upon the peasant masses below. However, the backbone of that revolution, which was to cost at least five million lives (and probably many more), was not the force of Red bayonets. Given the nature of a guerrilla war that comprised hundreds of thousands of little battles all over the countryside, probably no army of any reasonable size could have accomplished the task. Again party zealots were sent to the countryside, to organize the natural hatred felt for the relatively well-off by the poor, the down-trodden and the shiftless, to achieve the ends of the Party. Stalin's committees of the poor also used the *kulak* as bait, this time condemning them as the main hindrance preventing the less fortunate from creating the collective farms which would guarantee material security for all.

Mao's Point

American bombers over Vietnam may destroy Vietcong camps and cut supply lines, but the Vietcong guerrillas keep coming, and Western military strategists cannot agree on how many more troops are needed even to hold the military balance. Whatever the desired troop ratio, the crucial calculation lies not with the military but with the numbers of miserable, land-short, poverty-stricken and jealous peasants that are scattered throughout the country. If such people constitute the bulk of a society, or even a considerable proportion of it, a virtually inexhaustible supply of guerrilla troops are at hand for the comparatively few communist leaders to direct. Illiterate and insecure, jealous of their neighbours whose lot is not quite as desperate as their own, such peoples are potentially zealous recruits for the communist revolution, even though they have not the least notion of who Marx and Lenin were or what communism means.

As Mao proved in practice, receiving little Soviet aid in his peasant revolution, and as he repeated again in his latest interview with Edgar Snow, the military superiority of the enemy is relatively meaningless as a threat, and in important ways is of considerable value to the communist revolutionaries.[15] The more military hardware the enemy brings into the region the better, because captured arms are a major source of the guerrillas' supply. Some of the best officers on the communist side are those trained by the opposition who then see the light and join the revolutionary forces. Most basic of all, however, to Mao's book of tactics is the presence of a dissident peasant mass upon which a new local government authority can be built. In China, in the communist agitation, the place of the Russian Whites was taken by the Kuomintang. The 'foreign devils' were at different times the Japanese and the Americans. In Southeast Asia the 'foreign devils' became the French and again the Americans, fighting for their own colonial domination and supporting the local traitors, the Emperor Bao Dai, President Ngo Dinh and other puppets. In Asia, with the exception of the Japanese, the 'foreign devils' were more easily recognized because they were white men fighting and killing the yellow Asiatics.

The dates, places and faces change, but the problems and the tactics remain the same. Effective control of the village is achieved by stimulating the peasants' desire for land and their hatred of foreigners and finally by dividing the peasants themselves, depending on the poor to terrorize the rich. As Mao pointed out to Edgar Snow, his frank explanation of the communist strategy is really not listened to in the West. Therefore, given the communists' strategy in 'wars of national liberation' and their history of successes, unless and until Western strategists tear the blinkers from their own eyes and begin to provide genuine hope for improved conditions in predominantly peasant societies, hope that is directed primarily by native local authority, there will simply not be enough Western troops or planes to stop peasant revolutions organized by mere handfuls of zealous communist 'interventionists', perhaps more correctly, *missionaries*. In the Vietnam situation, American retaliatory air strikes to the North may have hurt the Vietcong a little, and the pace of the revolution might be slowed a bit, but such actions are essentially a case of fighting the wrong battles with the wrong peoples at the wrong time.

Of course, some morbid extremists, half perceiving these truths, conclude that the only solution is to obliterate Moscow, Peking, Hanoi and Havana. Even inhumanly assuming that such action was conceivable without equal devastation in the West, such insanity would not affect the conditions of the peasant majorities in Southeast Asia, Africa and much of Latin America. Even if the communist missionaries were to vanish from the earth, the techniques evolved by Lenin and Stalin in their organization of committees of the poor would hardly be forgotten.

Western observers of communist affairs have long recognized the essentially rural character of successful communist revolutions, but have not fully appreciated the techniques employed or the vitally important role of local government, probably because of their own political orientation, a way of seeing things that is completely foreign to the actual situation in a peasant revolutionary setting. Political parties committed to parliamentary democracy tend to focus their attention and their main effort on the offices of the national government rather than on the regional or local public offices. This approach stems to some extent from the historical (nineteenth-century) origin of parliamentary parties when power was mostly concentrated in the nation's capital in the hands of the monarch and his ministers and when the population was not directly involved in the political process. Also, of course, in the normal functioning of parliamentary democracy, a party must win a majority of seats in the national parliament in order to elect the chief executive and control the national government. The parliamentary democratic orientation, therefore, regards Paris, Peking, Warsaw or Saigon as the real source of political power and as perhaps the only place which must be watched and won in any political struggle. This is traditional politics for the Western state, but is hardly relevant to the politics of nations in the throes of agrarian revolution.

Under the changed conditions in world affairs, the communists often refuse to play the game according to the gentlemanly, parliamentary rules. Their prime objective is to capture power at the local level first, and then to use their base in the countryside for their attack on the capital. Their approach results only partly from their ideological commitment to the 'masses', the commitment which requires them to win the population not for parliamentary victory but for the communist faith; there are also strong practical motivations. First of all, by their control of local government, the communists hope to destroy the effectiveness of the national administration, to plunge the country into administrative and economic chaos, and thus demonstrate the weakness of parliamentary democracy. Secondly, they can face the national administration with the fact of complete control of the country, with the exception of the capital and perhaps a few major cities, and argue that since they will win in any event, the official power should be transferred to them, either to stop the bloodshed, or to prevent all-out civil war. On the economic side, the communist revolutionary leadership also fully realizes that the peasants are not dependent upon the cities. If the bulk of the population is peasant and thus the major enterprise is agriculture, the livelihood of those who comprise the revolutionary potential is largely a matter of local subsistence. The threat to block the distribution of manufactured supplies or to cut off the sources of electricity, so vital to an urban society, is meaningless in the countryside of China, Vietnam and most developing countries where the drama of agrarian revolution is played out.

CHAPTER 8

'What Is To Be Done?'*

COMMUNIST AGRICULTURE'S NEEDS

IDEOLOGICAL and political power considerations always have had and always will have an important influence over economic policy making, but they have often led to serious economic losses. If already serious food shortages are not to worsen, most of the countries that need to increase their food production, including the communist countries, must alter their agricultural policies in favour of more intensive farming methods. Intensive farming demands much more than increased economic investments. The availability in ample quantity of such aids as chemical fertilizers and tractors will not in itself assure high yields of crops and animals on the farms. Since the particular production demands of agriculture are fundamentally different from those of industry, output can be increased appreciably only through special organizational and managerial forms. Therefore, political, social and educational considerations are crucial in the search for greater food production.

False myths about agriculture have led to much nonsense in farm policy-making. One that has not yet been mentioned arises out of a belief that, if they are to be successful, farmers must love their land. This myth leads to the assertion that private ownership of the land is essential to efficient farming. Yet all over the world, and particularly in the United States, farmers achieve high yields of production on land they do not own. Neither love of a piece of land nor ownership as such can be demonstrated as essential to agricultural efficiency. What

* Lenin's famed question borrowed from the title of Chernyshevsky's radical novel of 1864.

is required, though, is a pride in one's work, and the feeling of personal accomplishment which is probably best represented by tangible economic reward from sustained and intelligent care of the soil and animals. In agriculture such conditions are probably much more important than in industry, for while the eight-to-five factory worker spends the rest of his life away from the work setting, most of the world's farmers spend nearly all their lives on their farms. Many farmers in America and in other nations do well on leased land and on land farmed on a profit-sharing basis with the owner. The highly productive though tiny pieces of land cultivated individually by Soviet collectivized peasants are called 'private plots' by Western observers, but this is perhaps a misnomer. All the land in the USSR has been nationalized. What the Soviet peasant does possess is less tangible but much more important: he has the confidence that the land he tills will remain under his and his family's control as long as he abides by the collective farm's rules and cultivates the plot efficiently, and he knows that the amount and quality of the produce from his plot, with which he may do what he wants, is directly dependent upon the amount and quality of the work he puts into the land.

In societies where food is in short supply, labour tends to be less dear than land, and farmers who have little hope of expanding the size of their farms make extra efforts to intensify their operations and maximize yields. Such is the case in Japan and Western Europe where most of the farms are relatively small, yet some of the highest yields in the world are attained. Whereas in Iowa's relatively land-rich and labour-poor environment the optimum size of certain types of farms is between 440 and 880 acres, in intensively cultivated Belgium and Holland it is probably much smaller. In both the United States and Western Europe, however, as has been discussed, optimum farm size must be related not only to the standard criteria of land, labour and capital, but also to the ability to make timely decisions. In Belgium, Iowa or the USSR this will be lost if a farm manager extends his operation to a point where he must depend upon a number of hired labourers, or peasants organized into huge brigades and paid on piece-work terms.

Workers on large-scale American corporate farms and Soviet state farms may get a little satisfaction out of successes achieved by the farm, but most such rewards will go to the farm managers, since they are the ones responsible for the overall operation and of necessity make the basic day-to-day production decisions. The average peasant can only heed the manager's orders and depend for the value of his reward upon the quality of the work of hundreds of fellow farm members. Of course, the salaried industrial worker finds himself in a situation almost equally frustrating, but it must not be forgotten that in agriculture worker attention, skill and initiative are much more crucial than they are in industry. One need only read of the back-breaking toil imposed upon the American itinerant farm labourers to realize that large-scale extensive farming, dependent upon numbers of paid workers, is one of the world's most degrading occupations as well as a disastrous waste of human intelligence and initiative. The American farmer has long recognized that the average hired hand is at best worth only a small fraction of himself. Since most successful farming operations, by definition, delegate few decisions, even the best of hired hands must be used primarily for physical labour. In the Soviet Union alone, assuming that the creative talents of the collective and state farm specialists (the agronomists, veterinarians, and other trained technicians who, along with the farm chairmen, comprise the core of the farm managing boards) are almost fully utilized, this still leaves scores of millions of collective and state farm members who are, in practice, in the same position as an American hired hand. Even though genuine effort may be made to encourage 'kolkhoz democracy', the several hundred able-bodied peasants who work on the average farm cannot collectively make production decisions in the infrequently held general meetings of the farm membership. The Soviet press and Soviet leaders have for years stressed the need to improve 'kolkhoz democracy' and to increase the involvement of the average peasant in decision-making, but, however well-meaning such exhortations may be, how can this be accomplished in practice?

Most of the collective and state farm officials we interviewed in Eastern Europe expressed genuine faith in the democracy of the general farm meetings or worker's councils, but requests for specific examples of how the individual peasant could show initiative always revealed that in day-to-day practice, he had, for the sake of so-called efficiency, to follow the detailed orders of his superiors in virtually all matters. It seems logical, of course, that the best-trained agricultural specialists should monopolize farm management, and inevitable that huge farms, to operate efficiently, require virtually as strict a discipline as does an army, but students of army life have long recognized that the price of discipline is a loss of individual initiative among the ranks.

Unfortunately, this initiative-destroying discipline stems not only from mistaken notions about the transferability of industrial experience to agriculture, but also from other ideological and political demands imposed by an authoritarian communist system. We would like to suggest several changes that must be made in the agricultural systems of the Soviet Union and Eastern Europe, if maximum food production is to be achieved. Most of them are fundamental, and as long as the societies' leaders and many of their followers believe that high levels of authoritarian controls must be maintained over the relatively backward peasants and that the peasants must work and live in ideologically prescribed collectives, changes that could remove controls and destroy the collectives are unlikely to be made. Yet they must be made if agriculture is not to remain the major, indeed, threatening problem area of communist states.

First, the false myth that industrial practices and techniques can and should be applied wholesale to agricultural production should be thrown out, and agriculture should be viewed as a unique kind of production requiring special techniques and methods of organization and application. Government leaders should re-examine their agrarian policies, correcting them wherever urban ignorance of agriculture has led to unwise decisions. In these land-poor, labour-rich countries every effort should be made to intensify farming, to draw out of every foot of soil every possible ounce of production.

Secondly, the USSR and the other fully collectivized states of Eastern Europe must disband the vast majority of the collective and state farms. Surely these farms are no longer needed as agencies of control. However unhappy peasants may be with the Soviet *kolkhozy*, they surely are as loyal citizens and as proud of their nation's successes as are the Polish and Yugoslav peasants who are predominantly independent farmers. True, disbanding the collectives would probably increase rural opposition to specific policies, but the economic gains and the gains in personal satisfaction to the peasant would outweigh any losses. By abandoning collectivization and encouraging intensified individual farming, the USSR might still be able to achieve the high targets originally set by Khrushchev for 1980 that would allow the Soviet people to enjoy Western dietary standards.

Thirdly, although Poland and Yugoslavia have been wise in recognizing that however desirable full collectivization might be for ideological reasons, the costs in lost production and peasant dissatisfaction would be too great, some fifteen per cent of these states' agriculture is still in collective and state farms, and with the exception of a few such farms for experimental stations and similar uses, most of them should be disbanded. Poland and Yugoslavia should work harder to increase the average size of their independent farms. Whatever one's ideological persuasion, there can be little disagreement that the present tiny farms averaging some three to five hectares are too small. They are further handicapped by government policies that tend to give the state and collective farms first choice of materials that are in short supply, and allow the independent farmer only what is left over. For example, Yugoslavian peasant farmers have been restricted from buying new tractors, and in Poland most of the scarce mineral fertilizer has gone to the state farms. Still, the record of the individual farms has been very good, probably better than that of the favoured and subsidized communist farms. The statistics from Poland proved the individual farms are superior to the state farms on all major points but small grains, and that one exception is surely due to the lack of mineral fertilizer for the individual farms. Would not scientifically conducted size and management studies reveal that the largest individual farms in these two states are the most productive of all ? The old landlord system was inefficient and unjust, but the Soviet experiment in making the state the active landlord has been equally so. Surely Poland and Yugoslavia could greatly expand their own production and set a valuable example if they would significantly increase the limit on individual farm size (in Poland 25 hectares, in Yugoslavia 10) and at the same time establish higher minimum limits. There is great justice in prohibiting the existence of absentee landlords in land-short nations. There is demonstrable economic value in not allowing farmers to depend on extensive hired help. Given the need for intensive cultivation, would not both justice and economic efficiency be served if the farms were of a size that could be most efficiently operated by a peasant and his immediate family ? Perhaps the only hired help to be allowed would be the use of extra hands (youths from the city ?) at the peak of the harvest season.

Fourthly, the governments concerned must greatly expand educational opportunities for their rural populations. Advances in American agriculture in recent decades could not have happened without improvement in farmer education. Many of the agricultural specialists now working as administrators could be most profitably employed as local advisers and educators for the farmers, and, like the American county agent, could disseminate printed information, conduct experiments with farming methods and with new seeds and breeds of live-stock raised under local conditions, and hold classes and demonstrations on every facet of farm life and management.

Fifthly, genuine cooperatives that involve independent farmers without destroying personal initiative should be encouraged. The Westerner who dreams of the preservation of rugged individualism by the American farmer must be sur-prised to learn that whereas there are only some 3,700,000 farms in the United States, total membership in farmers' cooperatives is twice that figure.[1] In earlier days, before the American farmer acquired his modern material aids, com-munity help in building a barn or threshing was the rule. Here again, the example of the Polish agricultural circles and the Yugoslavian cooperatives for individual peasants (where such institutions are not used as avenues of political control) are of value. We were interested to learn from an Israeli agricultural economist that the advisers they have sent on agricultural aid missions to several developing nations soon gave up champion-ing the *kibbutz* example when they realized that its success was probably due to unique Israeli conditions, and instead encouraged the adoption of cooperative efforts similar to those employed among Israel's individual farmers.

For the good of their own people, the communist nations must adopt policies that will make better use of their food-growing potential. Unfortunately, however, the likelihood of the USSR and her sister nations actually adopting the changes outlined above is slim indeed. As already indicated, industrialization of the countryside, mistakenly believed in the world over, is a strong Leninist tenet as well, and it is unlikely that his doctrine will be rejected. Collectivization is a basic part of communist doctrine and to abandon it would be to permit half of the Soviet Union's population to revert to a kind of 'capitalism', or at least to private ownership, a heavy price to pay. The most we can hope for is that something similar to the *zveno* system will gain favour and result in somewhat increased production. In Poland even officialdom has recognized the inadequacies of collective farming, and hopefully they will make some move to reduce the number of such farms, although since the 1968 invasion of Czechoslovakia even this seems unlikely. Officially Yugoslavia strongly supports increased collectivization, though privately there are some doubts, but in Czechoslovakia unless the invasion angered the leadership to the point where they will no longer follow the USSR's lead in agriculture, we expect to see little change. Advanced education for peasants will very likely be slow in coming, for education is costly, and the specialists will be kept busy supervising rather than teaching and assisting because they are key in the communist system of controls. Finally, it is to be hoped that the number and range of genuine cooperatives will increase slowly among the independent farmers, but the peasants are suspicious that they may be government organs designed to increase collectivization. Cooperatives could even offer an alternative to the collectivized nations if they decided to abandon their present system, but as already implied such a move would be considered a long step backwards and is highly unlikely.

In a world in which population increasingly threatens to grow more rapidly than food output, the nations of Eastern Europe and the Soviet Union are being doubly irresponsible in not exercising their capabilities to produce more food, irresponsible to themselves, and irresponsible to hungry peoples elsewhere. Indeed, nations (including the United States) that do not make their maximum contribution to the advance in world food output are guilty of bringing the 'world calamity' closer.

WESTERN BLINKERS

Former Secretary of Agriculture Orville Freeman was right when he said that the United States cannot feed the world, and the Swedish economist Gunnar Myrdal was right when he said that the mounting world food crisis demands that the food surplus nations greatly expand their production in order to increase aid to the hungry nations. Humanitarian considerations demand that the United States send food to nations on the verge of starvation. Pragmatic considerations of national self-interest clearly suggest that the likelihood of a Third World War and of further advances by totalitarian regimes are fostered by growing mass hunger in Asia, Africa and Latin America. America and other nations capable of producing food surpluses must certainly do all that can be done by way of aid, but the problem is so great that aid by itself can be only a stop-gap measure. Population control programmes and peaceful agrarian revolutions are essential if there is to be any progress. This is the point where the wealthy democratic nations can best serve both their own self-interest and long-term world needs, since only they have the resources for the necessary educational and social programmes. Yet, here again, false myths that blind policy makers from taking necessary steps have been a major cause of tragedy.

A peaceful agrarian revolution can take many forms. The key to the successes in Mexico, the Philippines, Formosa and Nebraska is that the changes made have fitted the needs of the land and the temper of the men who work it. However, for most of the developing nations beset by problems of land tenure, land reform is the first stage in a successful revolution, never an end in itself, and genuine agrarian reform, as outlined by Professor T. Lynn Smith, must follow. According to him,

1. A genuine agrarian reform should effect substantial improvement in the abilities, capacities, and performances of those who cultivate the land to bring them more into line with human potentialities.

2. Any worthwhile agrarian reform should result in a substantial increase in the amount of agricultural and livestock products secured from a given amount of land and the efforts of those who work it.

3. A real agrarian reform should result in the replacement of wasteful, inefficient, demeaning, and stultifying ways of producing agricultural and livestock products by methods of agriculture that are efficient, dignifying, or ennobling to those engaged in agriculture and stock raising.[2]

This book has concentrated upon agricultural failures among the collectivized communist states, for which policies rooted in agricultural illiteracy and political intransigence can be seen to be a prime cause. Ironically, however different the ruling ideologies may be, wrong Western foreign policies, especially those of the United States, can be traced to some of the same faulty myths that have worked such mischief in the Soviet Union. Not only have past levels of American agricultural aid to the developing nations been woefully inadequate, but much of what has been done has been rooted in a belief that American technology can solve the problems of backward agrarian systems. True, while it lived, the Alliance for Progress tactfully suggested that agrarian reform was needed in Latin America. But the masses of military aid sent to many countries, the American Marines in the Dominican Republic and the tragic sacrifice of lives in Vietnam, reveal that most American foreign policy is influenced by a false faith in an outmoded rural capitalism that was thrown out in America's own agrarian revolution after the disaster of the 1930s, but still compels it to repeatedly back regimes which rest upon semi-feudalistic agrarian systems.

How many times has Saigon promised land reform which has never been effectively carried out? How many Vietnamese and American lives have been lost, how many billions of dollars wasted, in a war backing leaders whose major support comes from landlords set against agrarian reform? As simple as it may sound, thousands of lives and billions of dollars could have been saved if but a fraction of America's wealth and man-power had been spent in subsidizing the purchase of the land for Vietnam's desperate peasant masses. Land redistribution in the developing nations may be only the first step towards achieving meaningful agrarian reform, but until it is taken, no reform of any sort can be achieved, and a Vietnam war cannot be successfully concluded. As desirable as an armistice is, it alone will not stop the forces of a green uprising in Southeast Asia. Elsewhere more 'wars of national liberation' will break out and mankind will move ever closer to the brink of disaster, due to a blindness shared by communists and constitutional democrats alike.

Notes*

PREFACE

1. R. M. MacIver, *The Web of Government*, Macmillan, New York, 1948, pp. 4 and 5.

FOREWORD

1. *Production Yearbook, 1965*, Food and Agricultural Organization of the United Nations, Rome, 1966, p. 20.
2. Theodore W. Schultz, *Transforming Traditional Agriculture*, Yale University Press, New Haven and London, 1964, p. 113.
3. John M. Brewster and Gene Wunderlich, 'Farm Size, Capital and Tenure Requirements', *Adjustments in Agriculture – a National Casebook*, Carlton F. Christian (ed.), Iowa University Press, Ames, Iowa, 1961, p. 207.
4. *Statistical Yearbook, 1965*, United Nations, New York, 1966, pp. 27 and 31.
5. *Agricultural Statistics 1966*, United States Department of Agriculture, United States Government Printing Office, Washington, 1966, p. 463.
6. ibid., p. 591.

2. THE POLITICS OF STALIN'S 'REVOLUTION FROM ABOVE'

1. *Narodnoe khozyaistvo SSSR v 1965 godu*, gosstatizdat, Moskva, 1966, p. 7.

* Unless otherwise designated, titles of Soviet articles in English indicate that we have used such excellent translation sources as the Joint Publications Research Service and *The Current Digest of The Soviet Press*. Often, however, the translation was checked against the original if this seemed desirable.

2. ibid.

3. Roy D. Laird, 'Soviet Agricultural Output in 1980: An Appraisal', *Ost Europa Wirtschaft*, No. 2, June 1965, pp. 90–104.

4. David Rybanov is credited with originating this description of the NEP. See Merle Fainsod, *How Russia is Ruled*, Cambridge, 1953, p. 97.

5. V. I. Lenin, 'Report Delivered at the Eighth All-Russian Communist Party (Bolshevik)', 23 March 1919, *Selected Works*, vol. VIII, New York, 1943, p. 178.

6. See, for example, V. I. Lenin, 'Report Delivered at the Eighth All-Russian Congress of Soviets', 22 December 1920, ibid., pp. 247–78.

7. See, for example, V. I. Lenin, 'Preliminary Draft Theses on the Agrarian Question', *Collected Works*, vol. 31, April–December 1920, Foreign Languages Publishing House, Moscow, 1966, p. 162, and his 'Speech Delivered at the First Congress of Agricultural Communes and Agricultural Artels', 5 December 1919, ibid., vol. 30, p. 196.

8. Fedor Belov, *The History of a Soviet Collective Farm*, Praeger, New York, 1955.

9. J. Stalin, *Leninism: Selected Writings*, New York, 1942, pp. 169–74.

10. See this author's (and his students') *The Rise and Fall of the MTS as an Instrument of Soviet Rule*, Governmental Research Series, No. 22, University of Kansas Press, Lawrence, Kansas, 1960, especially pp. 14–16 and 68–74.

11. ibid.

12. Stalin (?), 'Protiv izhrashchenii v organizatsii truda i kolkhozakh', *Pravda*, 19 February 1950, pp. 2–5.

13. *Narodnoe khozyaistvo . . . 1965 . . .*, op. cit., p. 257.

14. See Roy D. Laird, *Collective Farming in Russia: A Political Study of the Soviet Kolkhozy*, University of Kansas Press, Lawrence, Kansas, 1958, pp. 113–41.

15. See Roy D. Laird, 'Some Characteristics of the Soviet Leadership System: A Maturing Totalitarian System?', *Midwest Journal of Political Science*, vol. X, No. 1, February 1966, pp. 29–38.

3. COLLECTIVIZATION:
THE STRENGTH OF THE MYTH

1. MacIver, op. cit.

2. Alfred G. Meyer, 'The Functions of Ideology in the Soviet Political System', *Soviet Studies*, vol. XVII, No. 3, January 1966, pp. 273–85. See also this author's answer to Professor Meyer, 'The New Soviet Myth: Marx is Dead, Long Live Communism!', *Soviet Studies*, vol. XVIII, No. 4, April 1967, pp. 511–18.

3. Frederick Engels, *Anti-Dühring*, Moscow, 1947, p. 133. See also the discussion on this point in David Mitrany, *Marx Against the Peasant*, University of North Carolina Press, Chapel Hill, North Carolina, pp. 41–71.

4. V. I. Lenin, 'The Agrarian Question in Russia Towards the Close of the Nineteenth Century', *Collected Works*, vol. 15, March 1908–August 1909, Foreign Languages Publishing House, Moscow, 1963, pp. 129 and 131.

5. Lenin, 'Preliminary Draft Theses . . .' op. cit., p. 162.

6. ibid., p. 157, and 'Speech Delivered . . .', op. cit., p. 196.

7. *History of the Communist Party of the Soviet Union (Bolsheviks)*, Foreign Languages Publishing House, Moscow, 1950, p. 374.

8 J. Stalin, *Economic Problems of Socialism in the USSR*, Foreign Languages Publishing House, Moscow, 1952, p. 100.

9. *Pravda*, 27 March 1965, pp. 2–4.

10. V. Kulikov, 'Sovetskoe krest'yanstvo', *Kommunist*, No. 4, March 1966, pp. 91–6.

11. ibid.

12. V. V. Matskevich, 'Ekonomicheskie problemy dalneisnevo razvitiia sel'skoyo khoziaistva', *Voprosy ekonomiki*, No. 6, June 1965, pp. 1–13.

13. Yu. V. Arutyunyan, 'Sotsial'naya struktura sel'skoyo naseleniya', *Voprosy filosofii*, No. 6, May 1966, pp. 51–61.

14. M. Rutkevich, 'Izmeneniya sotsial'noi struktury sovetskoyo obshchestva', *Pravda*, 16 June 1966, pp. 2 and 3.

15. T. Alikhanyan, 'Initsiative-prostor!', *Kommunist*, No. 8, May 1966, pp. 20–26.

16. *Pravda*, 27 March 1965, pp. 2–4.

17. *SSSR v tsifrakh v 1965 godu*, gosstatizdat, Moskva, 1966, pp. 91–3.

18. L. P. Brezhnev, *Pravda*, 28 May 1966, pp. 1 and 3.

19. Alikhanyan, op. cit.

20. *Pravda*, 1 April 1966, p. 4.

4. SCIENCE AND SOVIET AGRICULTURE

1. A. Rachinskiy, 'Proceeding Scientifically in Developing Water Resources', *Kommunist Uzbekistana*, No. 11, November 1965, pp. 76–82.

2. V. V. Matskevich, 'High Stable Rates of the Development of Agriculture are Goal of New Five-Year Plan', *Ekonomika se'skovo khozyaistva*, No. 5, May 1966, pp. 2–14.

3. Joint Party State Resolution 'On the Broad Development of Land Reclamation to Obtain High and Stable Harvest of Grain and Other Agricultural Crops', *Pravda*, 19 June 1966, pp. 1–2.

4. 'Scientists Propose', *Pravda*, 15 March 1966, p. 3.

5. V. F. Krasota, 'Training Specialists in Agricultural Science and Production', *Vestnik vysshey shkoly*, No. 2, 1966, pp. 9–18.

6. ibid.

7. 'Meeting of Rectors of Agricultural Higher Educational Institutions', *Vestnik vysshey shkoly*, No. 2, 1966, pp. 48–50.

8. ibid.

9. A. N. Kosygin, 'Report to the Twenty-Third Party Congress . . .', *Pravda*, 6 April 1966, pp. 2–7.

10. Krasota, op. cit.

11. ibid.

12. V. Tomilov, 'Guardianship or Search?', *Izvestia*, 16 September 1966, p. 3.

13. Arutyunyan, op. cit.

14. Yuriy Shcherbak, 'Political Interference in the Biological Sciences', *Yunost'*, No. 6, June 1965, pp. 95–9.

15. 'Directives of the Twenty-Third Congress of the CPSU...', *Pravda*, 20 February 1966, pp. 1–6. See also Matskevich, op. cit.

16. G. Platonov, 'For Adherence to Party Principle in Science', *Oktyabr*, No. 2, February 1966, pp. 155–72. See the remarks by V. K. Shcherbakov.

17. P. Lobanov, 'Problems of Agricultural Science in the Five-Year Plan', *Ekonomika sel'skovo khozyaistva*, No. 5, May 1966, pp. 15–23.

18. Kosygin, op. cit.

19. L. I. Brezhnev, 'Land Melioration: . . .', *Moscow News*, No. 23, 4 June 1966, supplement.

20. Laird, 'Some Characteristics of the Soviet Leadership System', op. cit.

21. See my article on the *zveno* in the early 1967 issue of *Ost Europa Wirtschaft*.

22. V. L. Andonkiov, 'Population, Food and Land', *Prioroda*, No. 4, April 1965, pp. 54–63.

23. Stanislav Strumlin, 'Is Our Planet Threatened with Overpopulation?', *Literaturnaya gazeta*, 28 May, 1966, p. 4.

24. E. Arab-ogly, 'Scientific Calculation or Reliance on Spontaneity?', *Literaturnaya gazeta*, 11 June 1966, p. 4.

5. THE SOVIET TECHNICAL POTENTIAL: 1980

1. Lazar Volin, *A Survey of Soviet Russian Agriculture*, Agricultural Monograph No. 5, United States Department of Agriculture, United States Government Printing Office, Washington, 1951.

2. *Third World Food Survey: Freedom From Hunger Campaign*, Basic Study No. 11, Food and Agricultural Organization of the United Nations, Rome, 1963, p. 93.

3. Laird, 'Soviet Agricultural Output in 1980 . . .', op. cit.

4. Carl Zoerb, 'The Virgin Lands Territory: Plans, Performance, Prospects', *Soviet Agriculture: The Permanent Crisis*, Roy D. Laird and Edward L. Crowley (eds.), Praeger, New York, 1965.

6. THE PRICE OF COLLECTIVIZATION

1. *Pravda*, 18 September 1963, p. 1.
2. *Pravda*, 7 March 1964, pp. 1–6.
3. Brewster and Wunderlich, op. cit., p. 206.
4. op. cit., p. 120.
5. *Wskazniki Ekonomiczne 100 PGR 1964/65: Studia i Materialy*, Zeszyt 121, Institut Ekonomiki Rolnej, Warszawa, 1966, 46 pp. plus 96 tables, and *Wskazniki Ekonomiczne 100 PGR 1965/66: Studia i Materialy*, Zeszyt 141, Warszawa, 1967, 85 pp. plus 110 tables.
6. J. Kosicki, *Weilkosc, Gospodarstwa Uspolecznionego Ajego Efektywnosc*, Panstwowe Wydwnictwo Rolnicze I Lesne, Warszawa, 1961, 120 pp.
7. *Narodnoe khozyaistvo SSSR v 1965 godu*, op. cit., p. 87.
8. *Ekonomika gazeta*, 5 October 1963, pp. 21–31 and A. Esin, *Ekonomiki sel'skovo khozyaistva*, No. 12, 1963, pp. 16–30.
9. A. Strelyany, *Komsomoskaya pravda*, 15 October 1965, pp. 2–3. See translation in *The Current Digest of the Soviet Press*, vol. XVII, No. 44, 24 November 1965, pp. 14–16.
10. V. Borovsky, *Ekonomika sel'skovo khozyaistva*, No. 10, 1965, pp. 37–51.
11. Strelyany, op. cit.
12. *Concise Statistical Yearbook of Poland 1966*, Central Statistical Office of the Polish People's Republic, Warsaw, 1966, pp. 113–34.

7. 'A WORLD CALAMITY'

1. *Associated Press*, 12 July 1965.
2. *Third World Food Survey*, op. cit., p. 24.
3. *The State of Food and Agriculture 1966*, Food and Agricultural Organization of the United Nations, Rome, 1966, p. 17.
4. ibid.
5. *Some Important Issues in Foreign Aid*, Committee on Foreign Relations, United States Senate, United States Government Printing Office, Washington, 4 August 1966, p. 45.

6. *Associated Press*, 1 April 1965.

7. *Associated Press*, 12 July 1965.

8. *Some Important Issues in Foreign Aid*, op. cit., p. 45.

9. *Production Yearbook 1965*, Food and Agricultural Organization of the United Nations, Rome, 1966, p. 20.

10. David Mitrany, *Marx Against the Peasant*, University of North Carolina Press, Chapel Hill, North Carolina, 1951, pp. 205–6.

11. V. I. Lenin, 'To the Rural Poor: An Explanation for the Peasants of What the Social-Democrats Want', *Selected Works*, vol. II, New York, 1943, pp. 243–310.

12. M. A. Kraev, *Kolkhoznovo stroya v SSSR*, Moscow, 1954, p. 176.

13. V. I. Lenin, 'A Letter to the Workers of Petrograd', *Selected Works*, vol. VIII, New York, 1943, pp. 14–21.

14. E. H. Carr, *The Bolshevik Revolution 1917–1923*, vol. II, 1953, p. 157.

15. *The New Republic*, 27 February 1965.

8. 'WHAT IS TO BE DONE?'

1. *Agricultural Statistics 1966*, op. cit., pp. 435 and 467.

2. T. Lynn Smith, *Agrarian Reform in Latin America*, Knopf, 1965, p. 46.

Appendix A

to Chapter 5, The Soviet Technical Potential: 1980

1. Assumptions and conditions with which predictions for 1970 and 1980 grain yields were made are as follows:

a. The Soviet population will continue to grow at a rate similar to that of recent years.

b. No significant expansion of the crop area can be expected. Indeed the total area sown in recent years represented an over-expansion into marginal lands and reductions in the sown area were in order, as is shown in the post-1962 reduction in the area sown to grain (see Table 7 below).

c. Climate and soil conditions in the USSR are significantly worse than in the US. Therefore, although recent levels of American achievement were used as one of the yardsticks for measuring the projected Soviet potential, only a modest reduction was made for Soviet natural disadvantages. Indeed, since yield prices must be paid for the adoption of highly extensive agricultural systems, and Soviet agriculture is even more extensive than American agriculture, the ten per cent reduction under United States grain yields that was used was generous to Soviet hopes.

d. Although changing natural conditions can cause yields per unit of crop land to fluctuate greatly from year to year, records averaged out over several years give a fairly accurate forecast. While the bumper grain crop of 1966 (officially 170·8 million tons) actually slightly surpassed the new 1970 goal of 167 million tons, the average output for the four years 1963–6 is only 137·9 million tons (see Tables 6 and 7 below).

e. Most important of all, the future output of grain will be the major determinant of Soviet agricultural success between now and 1980. Not only is grain the source of bread, and bread is much more important in the Soviet diet than it is in the West, but grain increases are the major potential source of increased animal feed. Therefore, the grain potential is the prime indicator for measuring any possible future advance in the protein level of the Soviet diet. However, other sources of animal feed are important, and the original projection also allowed for a generous increase from such sources.

As Carl Zoerb has shown, much of the new lands area, which is largely in Kazakhstan, is very similar in climate to Saskatchewan, Canada, where extensive fallowing is practised. Therefore part of the present projection is based upon the assumption that the Soviets ought to be able to achieve Saskatchewan output levels on extensively fallowed new lands fields by 1980. Secondly, although corn was greatly over-expanded under Khrushchev, this crop can be profitably grown in limited areas of the USSR. Therefore, making a generous allowance for the total area that might be profitably sown to this crop, part of the projection is based upon the assumption that in such a limited area the Soviets ought to be able to achieve American corn yields by the Khrushchev target date. Finally, after assuming liberal increases in yields of other fodder crops in order to account for the total land potential, the projection rests on the assumption that since small grains sown in the long-established farming areas must be the major source of any agricultural advance, yields in these areas could equal 90 per cent of small grain yields in the United States. Therefore, as noted earlier, only a modest ten per cent reduction is made in this part of the projection to allow for the less favourable growing conditions in the Soviet Union. Such a projection implies an annual average grain production of 214 million metric tons by 1980 as contrasted with Khrushchev's original goal of 300 million metric tons. As indicated earlier, the implied achievement for 1970 in this projection is some 165 to 170 million tons, which is quite in line with the much more modest goal, implied by the new leaders, of some 167 million tons, but would not provide the additional animal feed needed to increase meat and milk production.

2. Key tables presented in the original study (and partially brought up to date here) are as follows:

Table 6

1956–62 AND 1963–6 ANNUAL OUTPUT
AND PLAN GOALS: KEY COMMODITIES
(millions of tons)

	Actual[1]		Plan	
	1956–62 (Average)	1963–6 (Average)	1970	1980[2]
Grain (official)	126	137·9	229[2] v. 167[3]	295–311
Grain (adjusted)	117[4]	124·1[5]		
Meat (official)	8·2	9·8	25[2] v. 11[3]	30–32
Milk (official)	58·9	65·8	135[2] v. 78[3]	170–180

1. *Sel'skoe khozyaistvo SSSR*, gosstatizdat, Moskva, 1960, pp. 202–3 and 462, *Narodnoe khozyaistvo SSSR v 1961 godu*, gosstatizdat, Moskva, 1962, pp. 300–301, *SSSR v tsifrakh v 1962 godu*, gosstatizdat, Moskva, 1963, pp. 140–41, *Narodnoe khozyaistvo SSSR v 1962 godu*, gosstatizdat, Moskva, 1963, p. 308, *Narodnoe khozyaistvo SSSR v 1965 godu*, gosstatizdat, Moskva, 1966, pp. 262–4, *Pravda*, 29 January 1967, pp. 1–2, and A. N. Kosygin, *Pravda*, 6 April 1966, pp. 2–7.

2. N. S. Khrushchev, *Stroitelstvo kommunizma v SSSR i razvitie sel'skokhozyaistva*, gosstatizdat, Moskva, 1962, vol. 6, p. 357, and vol. 3, p. 410.

3. New 1970 goals (e.g., average annual output for 1966–70). See A. N. Kosygin, *Pravda*, 6 April 1966, pp. 2–7.

4. The percentage reductions used by Professor Arcadius Kahan in his estimate of the gross output of grain for 1956–60 have been employed here. However, whereas Kahan employs a 10 per cent reduction below official claims for the years 1958–60, reflecting the 1960 revelation of increased falsification in reporting of output by the farms, a 15 per cent reduction is employed for the years 1961 and 1962. Moreover, while Kahan excluded immature corn that was counted as grain, this is included in the 1956–62 figures. See Arcadius Kahan, 'Soviet Statistics of Agricultural Output', *Soviet Agricultural and Peasant Affairs*, Roy D. Laird (ed.), University of Kansas Press, 1963, pp. 134–60.

5. 10 per cent reduction, and excluding immature corn.

Table 7

ALL GRAINS[1]: HECTARES, TONS AND YIELDS

	1953	1956	1957	1958	1959	1960	1961	1962	1963	1964	1965	1966
Hectares (millions)	106·7[1]	128·3[2]	124·6[2]	125·2[2]	119·7[2]	121·7[2]	128·3[2]	135·9[2]	130[5]	133·3[5]	128[5]	126[6]
Tons (official, millions)	82·5[7]	127·6[7]	105[7]	141[7]	125·9[7]	134·4[8]	138[9]	147·5[9]	107·5[5]	152·2[5]	121·1[5]	170·8[6]
Yields (centners per hectare, official)	7·8[10]	10[10]	8·4[10]	11·3[10]	10·5[10]	11[11]	10·8[11]	10·9[11]	8·3[5]	11·4[5]	9·5[5]	13·5[13]
Tons (adjusted, millions)	82·5[7]	114·8[14]	97·6[14]	127·1[14]	113·3[14]	121[14]	117·3[14]	125·4[14]	96·7[14]	136·9[14]	109·2[14]	153·7[14]
Yields (centners per hectare, adjusted)	7·8[10]	8·9[13]	7·8[13]	10·2[13]	9·3[13]	9·9[13]	9·1[13]	9·2[13]	7·5[13]	10·3[13]	8·6[13]	12·3[13]

1. Through 1962 including, and after 1962 excluding, immature corn counted as grain.
2, 7, 10. *Sel'skoe khozyaistvo SSSR*, gosstatizdat, Moskva, 1960. 2 = p. 127, 7 = pp. 202–3, 10 = p. 196.
3, 8, 11. *Narodnoe khozyaistvo SSSR v 1961 godu*, gosstatizdat, Moskva, 1962. 3 = p. 311, 8 = p. 300, 11 = pp. 302–3.
4, 9, 12. *SSSR v tsifrakh v 1962 godu*, gosstatizdat, Moskva, 1963. 4 = p. 137, 9 = pp. 140–41, 12 = pp. 144–5.
5. *Narodnoe khozyaistvo SSSR v 1965 godu*, gosstatizdat, Moskva, 1966, pp. 262, 263, 284.
6. *Pravda*, 29 January 1967, pp. 1–2.
13. Calculated from tons and hectares.
14. See Table 6, note 4.

Table 8

GRAIN *v*. POPULATION: 1956–62 AND 1980

	1956–62	1980
Grain (official annual average, millions of tons)	126[1]	300[2] (Plan)
Grain (adjusted annual average, millions of tons)	117[1]	214[3] (Technically possible)
Population (1959, millions)	208·8[4]	285[4]
Kgs per person (official)	600[5]	1,050[5] (Plan)
Kgs per person (adjusted)	560[5]	750[5] (Technically possible)

1. See Table 7.
2. See Table 6.
3. See pp. 138–9 and Chapter 5 above.
4. *SSSR v tsifrakh v 1962 godu*, gosstatizdat, Moskva, 1963, p. 10. The 1980 projection was based upon the continuation of the population growth of some 3·5 million persons a year that prevailed for several years.
5. Calculated.

Table 9

MEAT AND MILK: 1956–62, 1963–6 v. 1980

| | Official annual average | | | 1980: Plan | | 1980: Technically possible | |
| | 1956–62 | | 1963–6 | | | | |
	Tons (millions)	Per capita (kilograms)	Tons (millions)	Tons (millions)	Per capita (kilograms)	Tons (millions)	Per capita (kilograms)
Meat	8.2[1]	39.3[2]	9.8[3]	30–32[4]	109[2]	15[5]	53
Milk	58.9[1]	282[2]	65.8[3]	170–80[4]	615[5]	80[5]	282
Population	1959: Actual 208.8[6]			1980: Projected 285[6]			

1. *Narodnoe khozyaistvo SSSR v 1960 godu*, gosstatizdat, Moskva, 1961, p. 462, and *Narodnoe khozyaistvo SSSR v 1962 godu*, gosstatizdat, Moskva, 1963, p. 308.

2. Calculated from 1959 population and 1980 projection.

3. *Narodnoe khozyaistvo SSSR v 1965 godu*, gosstatizdat, Moskva, 1966, pp. 372–8 and *Pravda*, 29 January 1967, pp. 1–2.

4. See Table 6, note 2.

5. Increases are estimated in grain and non-grain sources of feed, but since even this would fall far short of needs, the author arbitrarily chose to apply the bulk of the increases to meat, thus milk is kept (for present purposes) at the 1956–62 level.

6. See Table 8, note 4.

Appendix B

to Chapter 6, The Price of Collectivization

The tables that follow summarize some of the more important of the authors' analyses of the extensive data gathered by the Polish Institute of Agricultural Economics on 100 representative PGR for the agricultural years 1964–5 and 1965–6.

In the Institute's attempt to maintain the representative nature of the sample of state farms taken from throughout Poland, some farms are dropped and others added from year to year. Similarly, because of changes in size (as when a farm purchases more land) the relative position of some farms also changed between 1964–5 and 1965–6. The farms are selected evenly from two major regions, fifty from the western and northern region and fifty from the central and southern region. Those in the first region were labelled as having somewhat lower, and those in the second region somewhat higher, costs. Within each of the two regions, the farms are again divided into groups of twenty-five according to size. In the central and southern regions twenty-five of the farms are under, and twenty-five are over, 450 hectares in size. In the northern and western regions the dividing point is 600 hectares.

Preliminary analyses of the farms within each region revealed a pattern of differences as related to size that is reflected in the tables that follow. To illustrate this, the hundred farms, which range from 159 hectares to 1,285 hectares, have been divided into groups of ten, graded according to size. The tables give the average size of each group, and the average figures for the two crop years.

All the farms have cattle, and all milk their cows. All the farms devote much of their sown area to some (or all) of the four small grains, wheat, oats, barley and rye. All the farms devote an important part of their sown area to sugar beets or potatoes and most of them cultivate both. Poland's terrain and climate are quite homogeneous, but some regional differences, particularly in soil quality,* do exist. Therefore, when the farms were divided into the ten different size groups, the smallest group of farms was found to have an advantage over the others in soil quality. They also had more mineral fertilizer available per hectare of utilized land. How much this represents government policy, and how much it reflects greater managerial attention to this matter, probably cannot be determined. Therefore, a control group was created. From the remaining ninety farms (i.e., excluding the ten smallest) the ten farms with the most fertilizer were selected, as were the ten farms having the best soil.† In terms of size, this control group proved to be slightly smaller than the average of the hundred farms (502 *v.* 562 utilized hectares). However, the average soil quality in the control group exactly equalled that of the smallest ten farms,‡ and the fertilizer available per hectare exceeded that of the smallest ten (162 *v.* 152 kilograms per hectare). Therefore, as discussed in Chapter 6, any distortion that might arise from comparing yields and profits of the smallest farms with the balance of the farms does not exist when comparisons are made with the control group, as shown in the final column in the tables.

Finally, we would repeat our agreement with Professor Shultz's implication that there is nothing magic about size in itself. As illustrated in the graph presented in Chapter 6, in Dr Kosicki's study yields of small grains in his Group III equalled that of his Group I. Similarly, in our analysis the Group 2 farms shown

* All the farms have had soil surveys, and are classified according to soil quality (rated 1 to 3) and the percentage of the land with the better than average soil.

† In this selection some overlapping (thus double counting) resulted, since some of the farms with the best soil also had the most fertilizer.

‡ In selecting the farms with the best soils for the control group, the farms with the greatest percent of their soil in the best of six possible soil classes were given first priority. Thus, when compared with the smallest farms the control group had 79 per cent of their soil in the best three classes, while the smallest farms had 77 per cent of their soil in the best three classes.

below kept more animals, the Group 4 farms had slightly higher sugar beet yields and the Group 7 farms had slightly higher potato yields than the Group 1 farms, but on all counts taken together the smallest farms clearly prove to represent the optimum size of the hundred representative farms. Most importantly, however, as stressed in the text of Chapter 6, management's ability to cope efficiently with its production responsibilities, and not size as such, is the key factor involved.

Table 10

I: FARM SIZE
(utilized hectares)

	I	2	3	4	5	6
1. Range	159 to 284	316 to 382	382 to 427	433 to 478	466 to 527	509 to 585
2. Mean	225	349	409	452	496	543

2: PROFIT INDEX PER UTILIZED HECTARE
(zlotys)

	I	2	3	4	5	6
3. Range	—2380 to 3970	—2269 to 2211	—1108 to 2859	—1512 to 4301	—1608 to 2284	—3384 to 2312
4. Mean	1258	414	267	669	48	345
5. Index	100	33	21	53	4	28

3: MINERAL FERTILIZER
(kilogram per utilized hectare)

	I	2	3	4	5	6
6. Range	85 to 303	72 to 222	45 to 210	64 to 301	75 to 245	63 to 200
7. Mean	152	145	117	128	134	112
8. Index	100	96	77	84	88	74

4: SOIL INDEX NUMBER
(1–3)

	I	2	3	4	5	6
9. Range	1·7 to 2·7	1·7 to 2·9	1·3 to 2·5	1·3 to 2·2	1·3 to 2·2	1·2 to 2·9
10. Mean	2·3	2·1	1·9	1·7	1·8	2
11. Index	100	91	82	74	78	87

5: SMALL GRAIN YIELDS
(centners per hectare)

	I	2	3	4	5	6
12. Range	13·9 to 34·7	14·2 to 27·2	11·3 to 27	10·6 to 39·9	10·4 to 32·4	9·2 to 32·1
13. Mean	25·5	21·8	20·5	21·2	21·0	20·1
14. Index	100	85	80	83	82	79

7	8	9	10	All 100 farms	Control group
552 to 701	613 to 752	724 to 882	882 to 1285	159 to 1285	322 to 750
614	704	787	1043	562	502

—1419 to	—2052 to	—1296 to	—1832 to	—3384 to	—861 to
3758	1304	2785	1940	4301	2578
707	245	645	319	492	843
56	20	51	25	39	67

75 to 169	66 to 174	40 to 173	40 to 170	40 to 303	63 to 301
113	96	98	93	119	162
74	63	65	61	78	107

1·1 to 2·5	1·5 to 2·5	1·2 to 3·0	1·2 to 2·0	1·1 to 3·0	1·3 to 3·0
1·8	1·9	1·8	1·7	1·9	2·3
78	82	78	74	82	100

10·3 to	9·6 to	10 to	10·5 to	9·2 to	15 to
27·6	31·3	37	22·8	39·9	32·3
19·9	19·1	20·0	18·5	20·7	23·5
78	75	78	72	81	92

6: SUGAR BEET YIELDS

(centners per hectare)

	1	2	3	4	5	6
15. Range	147 to 357	131 to 434	159 to 334	128 to 388	128 to 367	180 to 383
16. Mean	274	253	241	289	260	258
17. Index	100	92	88	104	95	94

7: POTATO YIELDS

(centners per hectare)

	1	2	3	4	5	6
18. Range	130 to 294	108 to 251	68 to 208	94 to 272	102 to 276	100 to 270
19. Mean	183	177	158	169	165	160
20. Index	100	98	84	92	90	87

8: COWS PER 100 HECTARES

	1	2	3	4	5	6
21. Range	13·1 to 56·3	20·5 to 35·3	10·3 to 29·9	13·0 to 36·8	10·5 to 30·3	7·4 to 27·4
22. Mean	34·2	28·8	22·6	22·0	20·2	19·6
23. Index	100	84	66	64	59	57

9: MILK YIELDS PER COW

(litres per year)

	1	2	3	4	5	6
24. Range	2003 to 3983	1497 to 3055	1185 to 3450	2195 to 3497	1721 to 3841	1916 to 4275
25. Mean	3040	2568	2530	2852	2785	3037
26. Index	100	78	76	94	91	100

10: MILK PER 100 HECTARES PER YEAR

(1,000 litres)

	1	2	3	4	5	6
27. Mean (25 × 22)	104	74	58	63	56	59
28. Index	100	71	56	61	54	57

7	8	9	10	All 100 farms	Control group
123 to 419	143 to 359	147 to 355	113 to 388	113 to 434	131 to 388
237	242	238	242	252	275
87	88	87	88	92	100

124 to 258	103 to 278	79 to 258	70 to 226	68 to 294	94 to 243
185	173	143	163	167	175
101	95	81	88	91	96

4·9 to 29·4	9·7 to 31·6	10·0 to 28·2	7·9 to 26·5	4·9 to 56·3	9·0 to 42·3
17·9	18·2	18·7	15·7	21·5	24·3
52	53	55	46	63	71

1975 to	1972 to	1807 to	1931 to	1185 to	1977 to
3284	4085	3982	3401	4275	4275
2633	2706	2728	2806	2769	2961
87	89	90	92	91	97

47	49	51	47	59	72
45	47	49	45	57	69

II: ANIMAL EQUIVALENTS PER 100 HECTARES PER YEAR*

29. Mean	83·4	89·4	66·3	73·6	68·4	59
30. Index	100	107	80	88	82	71

12: ALL WORKERS PER 100 HECTARES PER YEAR

31. Range	12·4 to 24·6	10·6 to 22·8	8·1 to 23·6	9·3 to 18·5	8·6 to 22·4	7·5 to 21·6
32. Mean	17·2	16·0	12·8	13·2	13·2	12·0
33. Index	100	93	74	76	76	70

* Excluding workers' private animals. Cattle = 1, horses = 1, 4 pigs = 1, and 300 poultry = 1.

57·8	54·2	57·1	42·2	65·8	69·8
69	65	67	51	79	84

8·5 to 16·2	8·4 to 15·2	7·1 to 13·3	6·7 to 13·7	6·7 to 24·6	9·0 to 23·6
11·2	11·3	10·6	9·5	12·7	15·4
65	66	62	55	74	90

Bibliography

The following list includes most of the major Western works on Eastern European and Soviet agriculture that have been published since 1940:

Belov, Fedor, *The History of a Soviet Collective Farm*, Praeger, New York, 1955.

Bienstock, Gregory, Schwarz, Solomon M., and Yugow, Aaron, *Management in Russian Industry and Agriculture*, Oxford University Press, New York and London, 1944.

Dinnerstein, Herbert S., and Gourè, Leon, *Communism and the Russian Peasant: Moscow in Crisis*, The Free Press, Glencoe, Illinois, 1955.

Halpern, Joel M., *A Serbian Village*, Harper & Row, Evanston and London, 1967.

Jasny, Naum, *Khrushchev's Crop Policy*, Outram, Glasgow, 1965.

Jasny, Naum, *The Socialized Agriculture of the USSR*, Stanford University Press, Stanford, California, 1949.

Karcz, Jerzy F., (ed.), *Soviet and East European Agriculture*, University of California Press, Berkeley and Los Angeles, 1967.

Korbonski, Andrzej, *Politics of Socialist Agriculture in Poland: 1945–1960*, Columbia University Press, New York, 1965.

Laird, Roy D., *Collective Farming in Russia*, Social Science Series, University of Kansas Press, Lawrence, Kansas, 1958.

Laird, Roy D., Sharp, Darwin E., and Sturtevant, Ruth, *The Rise and Fall of the MTS as an Instrument of Soviet Rule*, Governmental Research Series, No. 22, University of Kansas Press, Lawrence, Kansas, 1960.

Laird, Roy D., (ed.), *Soviet Agricultural and Peasant Affairs*, Slavic and Soviet Series, University of Kansas Press, Lawrence, Kansas, 1963.

Laird, Roy D., and Crawley, Edward J., (eds.), *Soviet Agriculture: The Permanent Crisis*, Praeger, New York, 1964.

BIBLIOGRAPHY

Maynard, Sir John, *Russia in Flux*, Macmillan, New York, 1948.

Mitrany, David, *Marx Against the Peasant*, Weidenfeld & Nicolson, London, 1951.

Ploss, Sidney, *Conflict and Decision-Making in Soviet Russia: A Case Study of Agricultural Policy, 1953–1963*, Princeton University Press, Princeton, New Jersey, 1965.

Sanders, Irwin Taylor, (ed.), *Collectivization of Agriculture in Eastern Europe*, University of Kentucky Press, Lexington, Kentucky, 1958.

Schiller, Otto, *Die Landwirtschaftspolitik der Sowjets und ihre Ergebnisse*, Berlin, 1943.

Tomasevich, Joso, *Peasants, Politics and Economic Change in Yugoslavia*, Stanford University Press, Stanford, California, 1955.

Volin, Lazar, *A Survey of Soviet Russian Agriculture*, Agriculture Monograph No. 5, United States Department of Agriculture, United States Government Printing Office, Washington, 1951.

Lord Walston, *Agriculture Under Communism*, The Bodley Head, 1962.

Index

155

MORE ABOUT PENGUINS
AND PELICANS

Penguinews, which appears every month, contains details of all the new books issued by Penguins as they are published. From time to time it is supplemented by *Penguins in Print*, which is a complete list of all books published by Penguins which are in print. (There are well over three thousand of these.)

A specimen copy of *Penguinews* will be sent to you free on request, and you can become a subscriber for the price of the postage – 4s. for a year's issues (including the complete lists). Just write to Dept EP, Penguin Books Ltd, Harmondsworth, Middlesex, enclosing a cheque or postal order, and your name will be added to the mailing list.

Some other books published by Penguins are described overleaf.

Note: *Penguinews* and *Penguins in Print* are not available in the U.S.A. or Canada

E. H. Carr

A HISTORY OF SOVIET RUSSIA

THE BOLSHEVIK REVOLUTION 1917-1923
(Three Volumes)

The first volume begins with an analysis of those events and controversies in Bolshevik history between 1898 and 1917 which influenced the nature and course of the Revolution itself. With these in mind the book makes a detailed study of the actual constitutional structure erected by the Bolsheviks and their means of achieving it. Finally Professor Carr turns to the multifarious problems facing the Bolsheviks as they took possession of a rapidly disintegrating Russian Empire, and examines the solutions adopted by them.

The second volume – 'The Economic Order' – discusses the economic policies and predicaments of the Soviet régime. It shows how the belated attempts to end the revolutionary chaos in agriculture and industry were interrupted by the civil war; how this in turn led to the series of radical measures known as 'war communism'; and how, after the civil war was over, the revolt of the peasants against grain requisitions and the catastrophic decline of industry forced Lenin to execute the temporary 'retreat' of the New Economic Policy (NEP). The course of NEP is traced down to the price crisis of 1923 (the so-called 'scissors crisis'); and the volume ends with a chapter on the first tentative steps towards planning.

The third volume – 'Soviet Russia and the World' – analyses the complexities of Soviet foreign policy. These are due partly to Russia's geographical position as both a European and an Asian power, and partly to the conflict between an attempt to promote world revolution on the one hand and a desire to establish normal diplomatic relations with capitalist governments on the other. The volume deals in detail with the activities of the Communist International as well as those of the Soviet Government. It includes a bibliography for the three volumes of the work.